Get this.

Right here.

Distance Learning

sebts.edu/distance | distancelearning@sebts.edu | 1-866-816-0273 | Southeastern Baptist Theological Seminary

Many Christians hear the missional call, but there is still a mystique around practice. When missional practice is shaped by the Bible story, we begin to see every aspect of the world through the gospel lens, and our missional imagination flourishes. In *everPresent*, Jeremy Writebol models this approach. By retelling the bible story through the theme of place and presence, we can see the places we live through the gospel. We will see opportunities for sharing the gospel, and how the gospel makes sense of every aspect of ordinary life.

DR. JONNY WOODROW
Associate Director, The Porterbrook Network,
Pastor, The Crowded House,
Loughborough, UK

Jeremy is one of those writers that other writers want to be like. I know saying that he presents theological ideas in a fresh and new way is like saying a motel in the back woods has "clean rooms" . . . but in this case it's true. *everPresent* does something that most books don't achieve in today's theological landscape. Most focus either on who God is or what we should do. Jeremy's efforts start with who God is to walk the reader down the path of what God has done, who we are because of God, and then, logically and succinctly, points us to naturally understand what we are to do because of this. I highly recommend picking this book up to better understand both the why and how of the life of those that follow Jesus.

SETH MCBEE
Executive Team Member, GCM Collective
Phoenix, AZ

I talk with church planters and pastors every day who are struggling to create a culture of engagement among their church in their communities. In *everPresent* Jeremy paints a picture of the Biblical sending and practical living of sojourners dislocated by rebellion yet strategically placed for restoration in our homes, work places, social gatherings, and cities. This is a book that not only encouraged and challenged me, but that I will use to encourage and challenge those in my church with our calling to be everPresent.

JOSHUA HEDGER
Director, Center for Church Planting & Partnership,
Midwestern Baptist Theological Seminary
Kansas City, MO

The Lord Jesus calls us witnesses, the Apostle Paul calls us ambassadors, and the Apostle Peter describes us as apologists. Every Christian is a representative of Christ wherever they are. In Jeremy Writebol's *everPresent*, he engagingly writes about the believer's responsibility of living out and sharing the Gospel. It is refreshing, readable, thoroughly biblical, and very practical. Be prepared to be recharged and then go "rep the King."

CHRIS BAUER
Senior Pastor, Santa Rosa Bible Church
Santa Rosa, California

everPresent does an excellent job of explaining the gospel message as it relates to the places we inhabit everyday. As a homemaker I was given a new understanding of my home as a mission field to care for, train, and send my children to live on mission for the Lord in the places they will inhabit someday. I found encouragement for my husband in his workplace and challenges for my family in every visit to the coffee shop, the grocery store, and the gym.

JENN MOLEN
Homemaker
Wichita, KS

Jeremy Writebol's book *everPresent* gives a helpful introductory biblical theology of place. The first step in living on mission is to see opportunity in the spaces where you spend your time, or, before even that, to reenter those spaces with gospel intentionality. Writebol helps us see how God could use us in those ordinary, everyday places. I picked up the book to help a friend and found myself helped. I recommend *everPresent* highly.

KEVIN P. LARSON
Lead Pastor, Karis Church
Columbia, MO

everPresent

How the Gospel Relocates Us in the Present

Jeremy Writebol

Foreword by Jonathan Dodson

GCD Books is the publishing arm of Gospel-Centered Discipleship. GCD exists to publish resources that help make, mature, and multiply disciples of Jesus.

Copyright ©2014 by Jeremy Writebol

ISBN: 978-0615989020

Cover design by Josh Shank: RocketRepublic.com

for Stephanie, Allison, and Ethan

May the love of Christ be the ever-present reality of our lives together. I love you.

Table of Contents

Acknowledgements

As with any project, there is always a host of people that come around you to support and encourage you in the work. Foremost of them is my wife, Stephanie. Her encouragement and support of me in this process have been immense. She has given me time and encouragement through this whole project. Her insights have been useful and welcomed. I am grateful for her beyond words.

I am also grateful for the two churches that have stood by me over the last year as this process has unfolded. Both my friends in California at Santa Rosa Bible Church and my new post, Journey the Way in Wichita have been encouraging, receptive, and prayerful for me through this. Dara Bass, one of my friends at Journey the Way took the time to proofread and walk through each grammatical land mine I created. Her editorial work allowed me to get a clean manuscript to the rest of the team. I am particularly thankful for Josh Carrillo who read every chapter and gave me helpful feedback and encouragement. Friends like him are rare and I count it a deep measure of grace to call him my friend and brother.

The team at GCD is also to be thanked for their encouragement and support of this project. Brad Watson has worked so hard to encourage, direct, and pray for me with this. JT Caldwell and Brandon Smith came on board

Acknowledgements

and helped edit the project further and make it a better book than the one I originally submitted. Whatever is lacking or unclear here is the product of my work, not theirs. I am grateful to Benjamin Roberts for seeing my vision on this project and giving me a green light to proceed in writing it.

Jonathan Dodson was a significant help, encouragement, and coach to me through getting the book from conception to reality. I am deeply grateful for his wisdom and help in improving me as a writer. In addition to providing the foreword for this book, he challenged me to rewrite much of the content from the first run and as a result I believe a better book has been produced. I am grateful for people, like Jonathan, who challenge me beyond my first efforts to create and craft better resources for the church. I hope one day I can serve a young writer the way he has served me.

So many others have been encouraging, prayerful, and wise with me through this process. I am grateful for the body of Christ and the presence of God in working through this book. Most of all, I thank Christ for the gift of grace to relocate my dislocated heart and then allow me to tell people everywhere about his kindness. To him be all glory, wisdom, and honor forever. Amen.

Foreword

In our first year of marriage, it was not uncommon to find me steadily peering down toward my lap whenever we had guests at the dinner table. I had to be prepared. If the conversation remained superficial or became dull, I would discreetly turn my eyes from our guests, and to my wife's horror, begin reading the book of choice, placed carefully in my lap.

I was present but absent.

This is, perhaps, an apropos description of modern life. Head down and heart disengaged, our thoughts are elsewhere. We are, as Jeremy posits, "dislocated." Teeming with technological distraction, or simply absorbed with Self, we are often missing from the present. We have lost the wisdom of Seneca who warns, "To be everywhere is to be nowhere."

The consequences of dislocation often go uncalculated. Jeremy does some of the math for us. Our sense of place is, perhaps, the first to go. Preoccupation blinds us to the sights and sounds of our surroundings and, as a result, we fail to fully enjoy the gift of the moment. Our environments devolve into means. The inherent value of place is lost on us and, as a result, restoring broken places is often far from our minds.

Worse still, people are affected. In my foolish stints at the dinner table, I dishonored my wife and neglected persons sent to my home to receive hospitality and love. Fifteen years later, I've improved my dinner table conduct considerably, but face a similar temptation with the smartphone. Dislocation is now socially acceptable. Our children may suffer the most from our disengagement with the present. While we may scoff at the hippies who escaped parental duties in pursuit of a high, our substance of choice may actually take us further away from our children. Certainly, the substance varies from person to person. For some, it is accomplishment. Kierkegaard writes, "Let us never deceive youth by foolish talk about the mater of *accomplishing*. Let us never make them so busy in the service of the moment, that they forget the patience of willing something eternal."

Of course, the lure of accomplishment can be cloaked in the eternal. "Ministry" is not immune from our disease. What then is the cause of our illness? Dislocation from God. Jeremy cautions that "soul dislocation is terminal." This is true not only for us, but also for those around us. Our diversion, not only impedes communion, but also disengages us from mission.

We desperately need relocation.

The Christian faith possesses rich resources to remedy this crisis. *EverPresent* transports us to those resources with fresh language and focused practice. It signals profound hope in the incarnate Christ who affirms place, and in the dying-rising Christ, who relocates us back into the all-satisfying presence of God. We do, after all, have a God who is omnipresent, with us and for the world in every moment. Jeremy sensitively and prophetically calls us to join God there, in the present, for our flourishing and the sake of the world.

Jonathan Dodson
Author, *Raised?* and *The Unbelievable Gospel*
Lead Pastor of City Life Church
Austin, TX

Introduction

For years in ministry I've struggled with how to get the gospel to the lost. I've wanted to be a good evangelist and share my faith. I've wanted to help people who don't know Christ to see how great and gracious he is and come to faith in him. I've wanted to see new-birth, conversions, life-change, salvation, or whatever you want to call it. The problem for me, however, was that I was paralyzed in living on mission. I was stuck trying to wade through the mountain of techniques, methods, and skills required to find, invest in, and hopefully convert a non-Christian to Jesus. I was frustrated with my lack of ability and felt disobedient to the call of Christ to "make disciples of every nation." Theologically, I knew how it worked. God is the one who draws and saves at the declaration of the word of Christ. Practically, however, it was not happening.

As I spent time reflecting on my problems, I had to take a look at all the methods I was relying on to make me a better missionary. As I processed through the "how" of making disciples, the Holy Spirit brought into focus the real issue. I was lacking presence with unbelievers. I didn't know any of them. And they didn't know me.

Then I had a moment. A friend one day was pressing me on what it looked like practically to live on mission in the midst of unbelievers. We were discussing sports and how we can build relationships based around the common interest of sports. My friend challenged me to come up with practical ways that the sporting-life would transfer to Christianity. I had to admit, I was a bit stumped. The only thing I could come up with was the opportunity it created to be present with lost people. And that idea, of being present with lost people, became a watershed moment for me.

The watershed moment brought a further insight about the nature of God. He is a God who is present everywhere. Theologians have labeled this attribute God's "omnipresence." Wayne Grudem defines omnipresence: "God does not have size or spatial dimensions and is present at every point of space with his whole being, yet God acts differently in different places."[1] As I reflected on this truth about God, I had to move the theology of God's presence into the practice of my life. As image-bearers of God, we are called to reflect who he is to the world. This includes attributes like omnipresence. This is where the watershed moment was for me. How do I, as a limited, finite creature, reflect God's omnipresence? By being present.

Understanding God's presence throughout the Bible and our relationship to him as the ever-present God has transformed my understanding of missional living. Once I realized he is present everywhere, in and through his people, I discovered that the method for being on mission

---

[1] Wayne A. Grudem, *Systematic Theology: An Introduction to Biblical Doctrine* (Leicester, England; Grand Rapids, MI: Inter-Varsity Press; Zondervan Pub. House, 2004), 173.

to the lost was really simple. I had overanalyzed it. The method is: be present, as a Christian, with lost people.

My goal in this book is to help you see how being present in the everyday places we inhabit is missional living. You don't need amazing practices or innovative techniques to help you live on mission. If anything, I've already told you what the technique is. Be with lost people. Even that is difficult in today's world. We are promised the ability to be everywhere through technologies that replace face time with Facebook. At a recent birthday party for one of the children in my daughter's school, I observed several parents who were present, but they weren't engaged. They were lost in their smartphones and Instagrams. Even though they were physically in the room, mentally they had left it altogether. As we consider the theology of God's presence and place, that theological reflection should lead to practical application. My purpose in this book is to help you understand God more fully so you will live as his people more faithfully. I want to bring the technique of disciple-making down a few notches to show you how God equips everyday, ordinary people to be his "sent ones" as they live their lives in the presence of unbelievers.

I am eager for you to see God's presence in your life so that we can go and be present in the lives of unbelievers for the sake of the gospel. When this happens, we will reflect an ever-present God by holding out an ever-present gospel.

Part 1: The everPresent Gospel

Chapter 1
Location: Where Did Place Come From?

Where are you right now? Take a moment and look around . . .

As I write, I am sitting in a café on Bitting Avenue. I can smell the aroma of roasted coffee. I can hear the patrons of the shop discuss their lives, what they will see on TV this evening, the rise and fall of the economy, and who will win the Super Bowl. I feel the warmth of a heater turn on as it is an unusually cold day. Light streams in from the front windows and illuminates the orange walls to bring a warm, homey ambiance to the room. Latin American guitars and beats fill my ears as the music from the café stereo plays. The apple-carrot coffee cake I am eating has a sweet, buttery flavor to it. The padded chair where I am sitting keeps me comfortable but awake. Right now, I am in a place. There are specific and unique events happening in this space that are not occurring simultaneously anywhere else in the universe. This place is special. This place is one of a kind. This place is the only place where I can be in the world right now.

This is not true of God. The Bible tells us that God fills heaven and earth (Jer. 23:24). It says that the highest heaven is not large enough to contain God (1 Kgs. 8:27). Nor is there a single place in the entire universe where a human can go and God not be present (Ps. 139:7–10). The word "omnipresent" sums up this spatial reality of God. He is present everywhere, all the time, in every way. He is not limited by anything and is fully present wherever he is, which is everywhere. Maybe we should venture down the path of comparison. We'll start with God. He is immense and infinite. He alone can be spatially present everywhere all the time. You and I, on the other hand, can't even exist in two places at once. This comparison can be helpful to put us in our place. But we need more than just a reminder of how ant-like we are. We need to see the importance of our limitation and the uniqueness of our specific place. We need to see that we are inferior to God in our inability to be everywhere present. And yet the places we inhabit, and specifically our presence in those places, has deep importance. Maybe we do need to be put in our place. What if being "put in our place" isn't about being humbled to insignificance but elevating our vision to see dignify the places we inhabit; to see that our presence is valuable and deeply important. We need to talk about God's space and place.

The Creation of Place

As I sit here at the café, I am privy to some special things: color, taste, smell, feeling. I can see two musicians meeting with a local artist to discuss album cover designs. Various cars drive by in front of me. Occasionally, I see a biker, although the winter cold prevents this from happening too frequently. This is a very unique place. It is a very creative place.

Who made it? Why was it made? If we ignore the Biblical story, we don't have great, cosmic answers for these questions. But if we look at the opening pages of Scripture, we have a fascinating drama unfolding before us. The first words of divinely inspired writing from the pen of Moses declare that in the beginning, God made the heavens and the earth (Gen. 1:1). Location is created. All of a sudden there is the creation of "place." Place alone, however, is boring. We have heaven and earth. Two categories, two ideas, but not really specific realities. The story continues to unfold. God doesn't just make categories; he creates places. The earth is filled with vegetation, inhabitants, colors, creatures, textures, liquids, solids, atmospheres, environments—places. The specific place called the Garden of Eden is unique. There are places within the Garden. A river flows through the Garden. The middle of the Garden has specific and diverse vegetation. Four rivers diverge from the main river on the outskirts of the garden. They flow to places with specific names and specific features. Some of those places have gold, some have precious gems. Each distinct. Each unique. Each a special place.

God, who cannot be limited by place, creates multiple locations. He makes places. Each of them are as unique and varied as he is. All of them created good. All of them beautiful. All of them reflecting and imaging his creativity and his diversity. Why does he make these distinct places? He makes them for *himself*. He creates all the diversity of place and location, with all its varied colors and dimensions, to display his varied and multi-colored glories. The song at the end of the Scripture story sings praise to God because he has "created all things and by [his] will they existed and were created" (Revelation 4:11). The everywhere-present God makes places because he can't help himself. Place is an overflow of his creative glory. Worship is our response.

Does Place Matter?

Why does all this matter? Since showing up at this specific café, I have noticed the flow of traffic in and out of the store. The aromas that exist in this room now are especially different than the ones that were here a few hours ago. The sounds are new, different, exciting. The musicians are playing their guitars and harmonicas now. It is a new and different place than the one that existed an hour ago. This place is unique and one-of-a-kind again.

Place or location is created by God for his glory. That means that everywhere we go, every location we inhabit, every neighborhood where we dwell is made for God. It shows us a multi-faceted and creative God, a God who is so unique and innovative that one specific location alone could not reflect his glory well. Each place sings the glories of God. Each location tells of his wonders. Each address displays his majesty. Does place matter? On every level, it inherently must.

The way the glory of God is seen at the Grand Canyon is different than the way his glory is seen on Bitting Avenue. The majesty of God takes on a different view in Mumbai, India than it does in London, England. The worship of God sounds different in the jungles of Ecuador than it does in the high rises of New York City. Yet each place is made by his will and for his glory. Each place has a specific role to play in declaring the glory of God, and no one place holds a monopoly on the display of that glory.

This isn't to say, in some sort of pantheistic way, that God is in everything or that we each have to find our own way of expressing him wherever we are. Just as a diamond will refract light differently in different places, so God's glory is seen differently in different places. Some places reveal it better than others. We cannot dismiss the broken and dark places of this world. They do not reflect the glory of God well. It is difficult to see the mercy and justice of God in the slums of Rio or the prisons of Iran. Not every place seems like it is God's place. This is why there must be restoration. If every place is made by God, for God, then the broken places that do not reflect God's glory must be restored. It's for this reason that every place matters.

If all things are created for his glory and if all places should uniquely reflect the varied glories of God, then we are called to see our places (including our workplace) as places of worship. Our specific place becomes uniquely important to our lives because it is from this place, and this place alone, that we can magnify God and bring glory to him. I look at my friendly café and I wonder: "How is God's presence displayed here? How is this place reflecting his glory? Where do I see his fingerprints of majesty? Does the coffee, the conversation, the art, and the atmosphere reflect anything of God's nature and glory?"

Take a moment and look around (once again) at the place you are inhabiting as you read this sentence. How does this place glorify and magnify God? How does it reflect his multi-faceted nature? What do you see?

God has created this very place where I am writing. He has created the very place where you are reading. He has created it by his will. He has created it for his glory. Now, you might challenge that statement because you know some architect drew up the design for this building and a contractor came in and had carpenters, builders, electricians, and plumbers actually make this place. But under God's authority, using the agency of humanity, he created and holds all things together (Col. 1:15). Place matters because God made it matter. You might feel indifferent to this place right now because it isn't where you want to be or because it is somehow broken and in disrepair. This place might be a comfortable, quiet place for you right now. It might be a place that doesn't belong to you; you are a visitor in it for only a season. Whatever the situation, because God has made it and made it for his glory, you are suddenly in God's place.

The Transforming Perspective

For way too long, Christians have considered church buildings as "The House of the Lord." We'd show up at specific places and feel that God was, in some way or another, more present there than anywhere else in the universe. Christians have called them "sacred spaces." We'd return to our homes and workplaces from Monday to Saturday and believe that the "secular" places were the outskirts of the presence of God. Sure, we knew he was there at our homes or jobs, but not in the same way he was "there" when we went to the church building. God was there; we are here.

Funny, God doesn't think like that. He's everywhere. He's in your house. He's in your car. He's at your job. He's present at your local coffee shop. He exists in the slums, ghettos, high-rises, and cathedrals of this world. There is no place where he is not. That means the place you are right now is God's place. This ought to be a transforming perspective for us. Where is God? Here. Now. Specifically. Uniquely. The very place you inhabit is God's place. He is here, right now. The Psalmist wonders, "Where shall I go from your Spirit? Or where shall I flee from your presence?" (Ps. 139:7). Jeremiah the prophet asks if a man can hide himself from God (Jer. 23:24)? The answer again and and again is "no!" There is no where we can escape from God's presence. He is everywhere. He is here.

I wonder what it would be like if we had this perspective more often. How would it change the way we see our neighborhoods? How would we live differently in God's place? How would we work? How would we play? How would we worship? What would we do with the broken places within God's place? What would we say to the broken people in God's place?

We should begin asking ourselves these questions. Our perspective concerning our homes, workplaces, gyms, restaurants, parks, office buildings, theaters, and everywhere in between should be that this is God's place and God is here. When I see those places this way, I am changed. I want this place to be a reflection of God's beauty, creativity, majesty, righteousness, mercy, loveliness, and hope.

This place is for God. This place belongs to God. This little ramshackle café on Bitting Avenue is God's place. The room, the building, the place where you are right now is God's place too. Seeing place this way moves mountains.

Questions for Group Discussion:

1. How would you define God's "omnipresence?" What relationship does his omnipresence have with specific locations and places?

2. In what way does God's creation of place give importance and value to the various places in the world?

3. How does the place you are in right now display the glory of God? What does it show or reveal about him? What does it fail to show about God's nature and character?

4. How can you begin to view the places that you frequently spend time in as "God's places?" How will that transform the way you live your life in those places?

Chapter 2
Dislocation: Why No One Feels At Home Anymore

CRACK! As I stood on the sideline watching my buddies at football practice, I heard the collision of the linebacker and running back and I winced. GROAN. Instantly the head trainer and I knew that the linebacker was going to be in pain. Teammates standing over his body began to turn pale and motioned for us to hurry to help their teammate. Obviously he was injured, but from where we stood some thirty yards away, we could not see the nature of his injury. You may want to brace yourself for what comes next. The trainer and I approached the fallen player and began to survey his body. No blood was evident, nor were there visible wounds on his arms, head, or torso. I glanced toward the player's legs and noticed that something was not right. As his left leg extended from his body, it made a sharp left turn at his knee and stuck out away from his body. His lower leg and kneecap had been dislocated. The way his body was designed to hold together had been broken, and now significant body parts were not in their right place. They weren't even pointing in the right direction. My friend was going to have a difficult time walking with that problem.

Have you ever felt that way before? Dislocated? Nowhere feels right. Nowhere feels like home. You're not in the *right* place (wherever that might be). That feeling can be one of the most unsettling feelings in a person's soul. More than just raising the hairs on the backs of our necks or making us feel the turmoil of fear and anxiety, dislocation unsettles every aspect of our lives. My friend's dislocated leg was sending signals to his brain telling him, "Houston, we have a problem!" Similarly, our feelings of fear, anxiety, helplessness, worry, and every sort of disturbance of peace tell our souls that we are not where we should be. Think about it. You feel those things. Fear, helplessness, depression, anxiety, and worry are all pain triggers. While we might comfort ourselves that each of these "feelings" is natural and part of the human experience, we equally know that they really aren't the way things ought to be. They remind us that we do not have peace. They tell us that we are not where we should be. This is a problem. We are dislocated.

The Dislocated Soul

How did this happen? If anything from the last chapter is true, then how in the world can we be dislocated? This is God's place. It is beautiful and unique, displaying his creativity and brilliance. I'm in God's place. Or am I? Welcome to the world of dislocation. We look around at the world we inhabit and, if we're honest, it's not a consistently beautiful display of God's creativity and glory. Our location is full of injustice, war, crime, poverty, rape, hunger, despair, even death. If this is God's place, it sure doesn't match up with all the good things of God. Something is wrong. We are not in the right place.

We have to see the story truly to understand these disturbing feelings and realities. Our souls send us signals of pain, frustration, anxiety, fear, and trembling because they are trying to tell us that we are not in the *right* place. The diagnosis is that we have acute soul dislocation.

Before we answer how our souls were dislocated in the first place, we might want to know what our soul *is* to begin with. The ancients conceived of the soul as the immaterial substance or essence of a person. The Bible presents the soul as the created spiritual life of a human being (1 Cor. 15:45). It directs and informs the desires, will, and emotions of a person.[2] Our soul is, in my estimation, our spiritual relationship system. From it we relate to God and one another. This is the reason that our souls will exist forever, even though our bodies will die. God is eternal and he has made us to relate to him forever. If our soul is spiritual and immaterial this begs the question, how was it dislocated?

The reorientation of our story has to take us back to the beginning once again. The Bible story reveals that God really did make this place. He made it "very good" and filled it with a whole host of creatively and beautifully designed things (Gen. 1:31). He gave humanity the mandate to multiply and cultivate all he had made. All the things that contribute to what we call culture (art, technology, language, production, industry, etc.) were given validity

---

[2] W. J. Cameron, "Soul," ed. D. R. W. Wood et al., *New Bible Dictionary.* (Leicester, England; Downers Grove, IL: InterVarsity Press, 1996), 1124.

in the first words of God to humanity. God invited his creation, his people, to make his place their place. He desired for us to make ourselves at home in his creation. As we made his place our place, the intention was that we would display that this really was his place. Things looked promising for God's place and God's people. This was God's place and we were at home in it. It was our place, too.

Then the injury occurred.

It was really a deception that caused the acute dislocation of the soul, but it was a powerful deception. Scripture tells us that our first parents bought the lie that God's place wasn't really good (Gen. 3:1-7). He had held back things from them. He had lied to them about their purpose in his place. The serpent spoke a word to convince them that they could create better places. They would not have to settle for being mere creatures but they could be creators. They could rise above the image-bearers they were created to be. They could ascend the cultivation and multiplication of someone else's place to manufacture their own beauty, identity, and image. All they had to do was show God who really owned *this* place.

And so our first parents told God what they thought about his place. They set up shop and took ownership of the place God had made to display his beauty and glory. They evicted God as the owner and ruler of his place. This world, these many varied places God had created to display his varied glories and beauties, was now under new ownership and we'd make sure that this world reflected another story, another glory. Ours.

Many people read the events of Genesis 2 and 3 and think that God expelled humanity from his place first. However, we must understand that we were the first to evict God. We were the ones who dislocated our souls.

The Symptoms of Soul Dislocation

As my friend lay moaning and writhing on the ground, each movement of his leg shot a surge of acute pain to his brain. As he writhed in pain, the heightened level of it was sending his body into shock. If we did not stabilize him immediately, he might lose consciousness. The dislocated leg was telling his body over and over again that help was needed. Emergency Medical Technicians were called and arrived quickly. They couldn't relocate the leg, but they could dull the pain and give some temporary relief to my friend. This was one of the few occasions at my high school when someone was legally high. However, he needed more than pain relief; he needed restoration that only the doctors could provide.

The dislocation of our souls in that Garden of God inflicted pain immediately. As soon as the eviction notice was sent by God, our parents felt the dislocating pain of shame. Until that moment, there was no need to feel awkward or exposed. Everything was out in the open. But now things were different. Self-awareness was immediate, and, frankly, we didn't like the image we had of others or ourselves. Our shame didn't merely reflect what we saw in ourselves; it also reflected what we saw in others. As we heard others' opinions about us, our minds bent to feel the dislocating pain that we didn't measure up. We were an embarrassment to them. We became an embarrassment to ourselves. The blunt force trauma of dislocation caused the shock of shame in us. We were not all that we had come to believe we were–and we knew it.

To stabilize our sense of shock, we went looking for something to dull the pain. It would never fix the problem of our dislocation, but it would dull our senses enough to make us believe everything was fine. Our first parents exhibited this by hiding in the bushes. They tried as hard as they could to escape the reality that they had dislocated their souls. They tried to find little places where the rightful Creator would not be present or aware of their treachery. By hiding, they sought to escape what was real. The irony of their attempt at a hostile takeover of God's place is laughable.

We still haven't stopped trying to self-medicate the pain of our own soul dislocation either. We might not be as obvious as trying to hide in the bushes from the ever-present God, but we hide in other ways. Our preferred anesthesia is *diversion*. We have created various forms of soul distraction to keep us from facing the reality that we are dislocated. For some of us, our "hiding in the bushes" is really hiding in church buildings. "Keep your friends close and your Enemy closer," we say. For others, the diversion is through entertainment, pleasure-seeking, and worship at the modern cathedrals of human vanity and pride. We attempt to relieve the pain of soul dislocation by drowning our sorrows in drink or driving our lives with such discipline that all we do is work, work, work. Regardless of what form it takes, we all hide in the bushes. Sadly, the pain might be suppressed, but the real problem still exists. We are constantly trying to build our own little places we can claim as "ours," only to find that we aren't at home in them. We are not where we belong.

Undoing Dislocated Souls

If we, like our first parents, are suffering from acute soul dislocation, is there a remedy? Unlike my friend's leg, there isn't a simple pull-and-pop remedy that will reset the bones and ligaments and allow the healing to begin. Our soul dislocation is terminal. Death is the final and ultimate result of this sort of injury. When you think about it, death is permanent dislocation from the place of God. We wanted to be our own creators and make the location of our lives the grand narrative of history. We wanted to put ourselves at the center of the places we inhabited. It was a fool's errand that has permanently bent our souls away from God's good design. Is there any hope?

As God comes back into the picture to find his creation broken and his authority overthrown, he has some decisions to make. He will see if his creation even understands what has happened. Just as a physician will ask a patient with a serious head injury simple diagnostic questions (what is your name? what day is it?), so God asks Adam, "Where are you?" God isn't dumb or blind, unable to hear or see Adam and his wife scrambling around in the bushes. He is compassionate and loving, so much so that he must see if Adam knows where he is. Adam's response reveals the tragedy of his soul dislocation: in essence, Adam said, "I heard you in the garden. I was afraid. I was naked, I hid" (Gen. 3:10). The symptoms are all there: fear, shame, disillusionment, and death. At that moment, there is no cure.

The place of God had been spoiled. The creation of God had been deeply marred. C.S. Lewis perceptively commented that time alone could not remedy what had been broken. Evil had to be undone.[3] Time could not heal. The only way for God to undo the injury of our soul dislocation was to undo what had been done. The place of God had to be remade. The people of God had to be reformed. The presence of God had to be relocated. Everything had to be undone. So God did the only thing he could do. He dislocated his people from his place. We are not where we belong.

What might appear as a severe act of judgment was, instead, an extreme act of grace. They could not inhabit God's place anymore. The moment humanity evicted God from his place the location was spoiled. No longer was it God's place. It was bent, broken, and ruined. It only contained eternal death. So God removed our first parents from his place. They were placed outside of death so that God could bring life. He removed his people from his place so that he could relocate them back into himself.

The fact that this world where we live does not reflect the glory of God well is because our souls have been dislocated. We have done great injury by trying to take over God's place as our own. And God has responded the only way he could without destroying us completely; he has dislocated us even more. He has done this so that he might redeem and relocate us in Christ. Today, we would do well to listen to God's diagnostic question to Adam. He asks us, just as he asked Adam, "Where are you?"

---

[3] C.S. Lewis, *The Great Divorce (Collected Letters of C.S. Lewis),* (Kindle Locations 85-87). Harper Collins, Inc.. Kindle Edition.

Questions for Group Discussion:

1. In what ways do you recognize the dislocation of your own soul? How is that dislocation revealed in every day life?

2. Do you believe that this dislocation is a universal one experienced by everyone? Why or why not?

3. What are the predominate ways you personally seek to mask or dull the pain of your separation and dislocation from God's presence? Why are these these things ultimately insufficient and unhelpful?

4. How was God's question to Adam of his location an act of kindness towards him? How does that question prepare us to understand our need for help?

Chapter 3
Relocation: How Christ Brings Exiled Children Home

"Dad, let's be honest. I hate you and all that you've built and done here. I hate the fact that I'm your son and that I'm part of this family. I loathe everything here. In all honesty I wish you were dead so I could escape you and this place and go live however I want. Why don't you give me what I have coming when you die anyway and we'll act like neither one of us ever existed. I want you to die, I want my cash, and I want to leave."

With anger and sadness welling up in his heart, the father thought long and hard about his son's words. He wanted to bend the boy over his knee right there and give him a thorough lashing to teach this ungrateful son some respect. Instead he did something unexpected, even humiliating. Over the next few days ,he liquidated the assets that would have been given to this youngest son and handed him a cash-filled envelope. Before the father could open his mouth to speak, the son was out the door and gone. Maybe for good.[4]

---

[4] This story was originally told by Jesus in Luke 15:11-32

Exiled Children

Standing outside of the Garden, Adam and Eve looked on with a deep sense of regret. They had believed the lie that they could dislocate God and instead ended up dislocating themselves. No longer was there face-to-face fellowship with the Trinity. No longer were they enjoying the ample provision and benefits of God's kindness. Their work yielded nothing easily. Every aspect of their lives and their created roles with God and one another was immediately distorted. Death was the ruling force. Their dislocation was total and complete. Was there any way to get home?

If we're honest with ourselves, we understand their plight only too well. Nothing in this world, not one place, seems to be free of this awkward uneasiness that we really are not at home. We go to work and there is some sort of pressure and turmoil. We have yet to find that singular relationship that is always happy and perfect. Our homes and family life, even the best of them, are not perfect. Life is frustrating, vague, discordant, and broken. Even the best of days can be laced with the frustrations of our brokenness. Is there any way to get home?

The World and Our Forever Home

One of the predominate features of any religion, particularly the major religions of the world, is their viewpoint on this concept of getting home. For most, the endpoint is an afterlife location. Many people perceive that world religions are essentially the same because they all have an end place in mind that is much better than the one we have here. It is believed that Christianity, Islam, Buddhism, Hinduism, and any other religion have the same location in mind. In essence, we are all trying to get to the afterlife of "heaven" or "paradise" or "Nirvana," whatever each culture envisions and names that place.

While it is true that there is a shared desire for a paradise beyond this life, a distinguishing reality between Christianity and other religions is that we actually don't leave this earth. It is still very much our home and always will be. Instead of leaving planet earth for a paradise-place in an alternate reality, we find the Scriptures clearly demonstrating that God comes to this created place of his own, inhabits it perfectly, reconciles the people who live in that place, and ultimately reconciles the place as the perfect home for his children. This is the plot-line of the entire Bible. Paul unpacks for us the way the Son of God came into the very universe he created and sustains (Col. 1:15-17) to do the work of reconciling *all things* back to himself by his sacrificial death on the cross (1:19-20). "All things" includes the earth that we live on. This is why in the amazing vision of the end that the Apostle John is given he doesn't see an *Escape from LA* type scenario. He sees the return of the Redeemer-King in order to "make all things new" (Rev. 21:5). Humanity is not transported away to heaven, but heaven comes down to humanity on the earth. Christ descends once again, permanently, to dwell with humanity (Rev. 21:3). All things are made new, even this earth, and we will live in a perfectly restored, perfectly renewed creation as perfectly renewed beings (21:9-22:5).

Relocation: How Christ Brings Exiled Children Home

The fundamental dislocation that we feel in the here and now isn't relieved by our being transported away to a different place. It's not even relieved in trying to put a new coat of paint on a decaying building. The dislocation that we feel is only relieved by God himself being dislocated from heaven to earth to redeem his people and to restore this place. Everyone is trying in some fashion or another to attain the "heavenly-life" either in this world or the world to come. The question is how do we attain that life? How do we get to heaven? Or how do we generate enough buzz to get heaven to come down to us? The way in which we live our lives reveals how we believe that greater and better place is attained.

So how do we get home? How are we going to make it?

--

As the boy wandered in the direction of his home, he considered everything that he had done. Certainly there weren't a lot of favorable activities in his life to warrant his father's acceptance. Even if he was going back to just be a servant, he was skeptical that *that* would even work out. The life of debauchery and shame he lived was great. It was one thing for a son to grow up and leave the nest to "sow his wild oats." But the manner in which he had done it was the stuff of legends. The wrong legends, but legendary nonetheless.

He certainly wasn't going to be able to appeal to his father on the basis of his own integrity or goodness. If he was going to get even a part-time job on his father's land, he knew he'd have to work for it and work hard. He'd show his father that, while he wasn't worthy of being considered a son, he'd attain a good standing as a servant. If his debauchery was the cause of his exile then maybe by his dutiful labor would he could find some semblance of restoration.

Working It Off

For most of us, getting home is a matter of working our way back to it. Our view of our rebellion and rejection of God is that we merely need to replace the bad deeds we've done with better deeds that will balance out the scale. Where we might have been unworthy to enter heaven by our sin, for sure we can make ourselves worthy by reversing the trend.

So we work it off. This is religion. Like a good financial planner trying to help a person out of significant debt, we counsel ourselves to replace our bad spending with good spending, our rebellion with righteousness. Religious entities seek to help people do this by providing options for righteous duty. Go to Mass. Give alms. Serve in the church. Make a pilgrimage to a holy spot. Wash in a certain river. Get married in the temple. The list of options for storing up righteous merit is extensive. Somehow we believe that if we just do enough, there will be black in our ledger at the end of the day, even if it is just a few cents in the black. We don't even have to perform in the confines of a religious institution. Just do good things in general and righteous deposits will be made on a regular basis.

Except that the problem has not been addressed. For every good deed we attempt, we find our hearts still unchanged, still dislocated. The world and our progress in it are not getting any better. We're conceiving of our problem in the wrong way. This isn't just a job where, if we perform well, we get a raise and a benefit package. This isn't a bank account that either has money in it or it doesn't. The relationship we broke is a family relationship and it was a fatal break.

Trying to be religious in order to repair our irreligion doesn't work.[5] A new way must be forged to bring us home. A way we can't forge ourselves.

--

The boy was ashamed. He had deeply hurt and disgraced his father. The fortune he had been handed to live off of was squandered. His morality and dignity were all but gone. Instead of returning to a comfortable, familiar home, he was walking up the road in uncertainty and shame. The stench rising from his body was further evidence of his estrangement and the reproach he had brought upon his family. He knew he could not undo the terrible things he had done nor would anyone be able to forget them. He just hoped he could exist in a better place than where he had been. He had no clue how his father would respond.

As he walked up the familiar road through town toward his family estate, he could sense the glaring looks from those around him. They knew who he was. They had heard stories of what he had done. There was no way this son was going to come home. He felt the shame he had caused. He had the speech prepared for his father. He was ready to eat humble pie and accept what he had coming,

---

[5] I am grateful to Timothy Keller for giving me these categories. For more, see his book *Prodigal God*.

if he could only beg for a little job with his father's servants. As he walked, his head hung. Suddenly he heard a gasp from several around him.

He looked up, and in the distance he could see someone running. It wasn't the graceful run of a child at play. It was the hurried rush of someone eager to settle something. Fear struck his heart. The son saw his father sprinting toward him. He had picked up the corners of his robe and was in a full-out sprint toward the boy. Was his father coming to end the relationship? Would he be utterly shamed and even killed before the townspeople for the disgrace he had brought upon his father?

Before he could even answer those questions, he felt the enormity of his father around him. Warm arms embraced his shoulders. Wet kisses hit his cheeks. Tears fell down his face. As the boy tried to get his prepared speech out, his father hushed him, clothed him in the best robes, put an identifying ring on his finger, and announced "MY SON!"

In that moment, the son knew one thing. He was home.

The Way Home

If dutiful diligence in doing good won't help us get back home then what will? How can we have any hope of reaching our desired heavenly home? The answer to this is not within us. We can have all our speeches and duties prepared. We can try to clean up and walk uprightly before God, hoping to earn an audience with him, perhaps even gain some respectability, but none of that will tip the scales in our favor.

The only basis we have of returning home is found in God himself. How does he do this? He gives us himself. Just as the father in Jesus' story of the prodigal son ran, embraced, kissed, and welcomed his offending and estranged son, so God the Father has reconciled himself to us. How has he done this? He's given us himself. He's sent his Son to relocate us back into him. How does he do this? The Bible gives a few metaphors to help us see how Christ has done everything to relocate us back home.

The Replacing Son

If we are estranged from God, it is because we lack any righteousness to be with God. Our rebellion is an exercise in our own self-dependence. We've written off God's standards and, instead, created our own. When we stand before God, we fall short–bankrupt.

Furthermore, rebellion requires justice. As God told Adam, "in the day that you eat of it you shall surely die" (Gen. 2:17). So death has been the natural and perpetual consequence of our sins. God is right to send us to death. And in sending Jesus for us, he doubly replaces us.

Jesus stands as the replacement for our misdeeds by taking our sin upon himself. As the Scriptures declare, "For our sake he made him to be sin who knew no sin" (2 Cor. 5:21). He replaced us on the cross and took the just punishment for our sins. He died as a substitute for us.

But more than just standing in our place for our sins, Jesus also stands as the replacement by providing us with his righteousness. In him we are no longer under the judgment of God because of our lack of righteousness, but we are gifted the perfect righteousness of Jesus as if it was our own. The passage quoted above goes on to state: "For our sake he made him to be sin who knew no sin, *so that in him we might become the righteousness of God*" (emphasis mine). In the sending of the Son, the Father provides the righteousness we need and takes the punishment we deserve.

The Reuniting Son

Having a clean slate is good, but it doesn't get us home. We need a new relationship. And so Jesus the Son of God came as a reconciler. He came to reunite us to God through his work.

In Christ we are reunited to the Father. Jesus' ministry was more than just a mop-up job on a sin problem. His life, death, and resurrection were all aimed at reconciling us to the Father. If our rebellion turned us into mortal enemies of God, the work of Christ, specifically his cross-work, speaks to the reality that we have been reconciled to him. Paul speaks of it this way in Romans:

> *"For if while we were enemies we were reconciled to God by the death of his Son, much more, now that we are reconciled, shall we be saved by his life. More than that, we also rejoice in God through our Lord Jesus Christ, through whom we have now received reconciliation." (Rom. 5:10–11)*

Reconciliation promises to give us life. It promises the reversal of our state of death. No longer do we have to fear death. Jesus has taken death for us and has reconciled us back to God so that death is not eternal. Instead, he grants us life eternal. We will die once, but it will be a death to life. All of this is possible because Jesus served as the mediator to reconcile us to his Father. This reconciliation is a unification. Notice how Paul states this in Ephesians 2:13-16:

> *"But now in Christ Jesus you who once were far off have been brought near by the blood of Christ. For he himself is our peace... so making peace, and might reconcile us both to God in one body through the cross, thereby killing the hostility." (Eph. 2:13–16)*

"In Christ" we are united with him in his life, death, and resurrection and that unification kills the hostility between us and God. It also kills the hostility that exists between us and others, no matter what the distinction—racial, economic, education, or otherwise. Christ reconciles us vertically (toward God) and horizontally (toward one another).

The Restoring Son

One of the deepest metaphors for our relocation in Scripture is that of our restoration to God. It's not merely a restoration of all that was in the past. It is the restoration and renovation of all that will be.

In the atoning work of Jesus on our behalf, we have a substitute, a reconciler, and a brother (Heb. 2:10-11, Matt. 25:40). The restoring work of the Son is to bring God's *children* home. It's to bring us into his family. Theologically, this is the doctrine of adoption. By faith in Christ, we are no longer rebels, no longer estranged, but sons and daughters.

The gospel of God's grace is a complete restoration. It gives us one who substitutes himself for us, one who reconciles us back to God, and one who restores us back into the family so that we can rightly call God our Father once again. Like the prodigal son, we might feel that asking God for full rights as his children is a step too far. We're content to simply be tolerated by God , and labor on as unworthy servants. But God's grace goes so much further than we could ever plan or expect. He doesn't want to reconcile mere servants. He wants to restore children.

So the Scriptures tell us:

"But when the fullness of time had come, God sent forth his Son, born of woman, born under the law, to redeem those who were under the law, so that we might receive adoption as sons. And because you are sons, God has sent the Spirit of his Son into our hearts, crying, "Abba! Father!" So you are no longer a slave, but a son, and if a son, then an heir through God." (Gal. 4:4–7)

The life, death, and resurrection of Jesus weren't merely about a substitution, although a substitution was necessary. Nor was it about a legal reconciliation, even though that was required. The sending of the Son was for our adoption. It was to bring dislocated, exiled children back home. The love of our Father is so great that he had to run to us, cleanse us, identify us as his own, and proclaim "MY SON!"

How Do We Get Home?

Every religion in the world is constructing systems and paradigms to get us home. The reality, however, is that none of them work. None of them can adequately do the job of restoring the dislocating reality of our sin. They put all the requirements for salvation on us. Shouldered with burdens of religious performance to either satisfy a deity that can't be satisfied or to find a state of transcendental enlightenment, it is no wonder no one feels that they can make it to the heavenly paradise they so desire.

And yet, that's exactly how the good news of the gospel of Jesus helps us. We can't go to God. He comes to us. He sends himself for us as the shepherd who goes after the lost sheep. He's the father running to find his lost child. He's the one who does it all to bring us home.

How do we get home? We get home by way of Jesus. He has done everything to bring his dislocated brothers and sisters back to the Father.

Questions for Group Discussion:

1. In what ways are we like the exiled son with his father and Adam and Eve with God in our separation from God? How do we attempt to fix our brokenness?

2. Why is religious performance unable to fix an irreligious life? How do we attempt to fix our brokenness by doing religious duties?

3. How is Christ's dislocation from heaven to earth able to relocate us from exiled to redeemed? Why is this good news?

4. Why do we need Jesus' replacing, reuniting and restoring work? What happens if we have any one of these components with out the others?

Chapter 4
Renovation: Why the Places We Live Are Important

Renovation projects are not easy. I know a few friends who have tried their hand at flipping homes. They purchase an decent yet substandard home, put some labor and money into the place to update features and improve the structures of the home, and then turn around and sell the place for more than they initially invested. It sounds pretty easy on paper, especially if you have the initial capital on hand to make it work. But if you're doing it on a budget, by yourself, then making it work can be a real trick. It requires a lot of effort.

The work we've put into renovating certain aspects of our home has been substantial, especially for someone like me who has no experience in home repair. The basement, bathrooms, front lawn, kitchen floor, and aesthetic of the inside and outside of our home have undergone major makeovers. Sometimes Stephanie and I look at one another and wonder just what we were thinking when we bought this particular home. Why would we buy a place that we'd have to spend so much time and energy renovating?

Material vs. Spiritual, the Unnecessary Dichotomy

The claims of the gospel are spiritual in nature. They deal with our inner lives, our heart and soul, and relate us to a God who is Spirit. The gospel enables us to relate to God spiritually, but that's not all. The gospel also makes very concrete claims. However, these physical claims, clearly observed in God also becoming flesh, are often neglected. This is due, in part, to certain philosophical influences upon the Christian faith. Plato advocated a dualism that compartmentalized spiritual and physical. He conceived the idea that every material object in this world was the lesser copy of a supreme idea or "form" that was spiritual or non-material. In his thought, the spiritual "forms" are superior to their lesser reflections in the physical world. The Platonic hope was to escape the physical world in order to become a philosopher-king, enthroned in philosophical reflection.[6] This pattern of thinking led to a devaluing of the material world. In some strands of Greek philosophy, the material was not only inferior but also the location of evil and corruption.[7] Platonists argued that the body contained insatiable desires and lusts that destroy and contaminate the entire person (body and soul). As a result, they believed the body would

---

[6] J. M. Dillon, "Plato, Platonism," ed. Craig A. Evans and Stanley E. Porter, *Dictionary of New Testament Background: a Compendium of Contemporary Biblical Scholarship* (Downers Grove, IL: InterVarsity Press, 2000), 805.

[7] "Probably the foundational conviction of the Gnostics is the commitment to a radical anticosmic dualism in which all that is material—the world and the body—is seen as evil." D. M. Scholer, "Gnosis, Gnosticism, ed. Ralph P. Martin and Peter H. Davids, *Dictionary of the Later New Testament and Its Developments,* (Downers Grove, IL: InterVarsity Press, 1997).

be done away with at its death. Only the immaterial soul or spirit would remain. They contended that the eternal part of our humanity was the more important, spiritual side.[8]

Several Christian cults took this kind of philosophy pretty far. They introduced unbiblical ideas such as: the rejection of the incarnation, Jesus possessing an actual physical body and the denial of the resurrection, a physical resurrection of the body. They spiritualized Jesus and the resurrection. Early Church councils worked hard to extract Greek philosophy from biblical theology, concluding that the gospel affirms both the spiritual and material. In general, they concluded that body and spirit are both real and good, but both had also been corrupted by the fall of man.[9]

Even though church councils have affirmed the value of both the physical and spiritual aspects of the human body, the division between spiritual and material in relationship to our places still exists. This imbedded aspect of Western philosophy still exerts an influence upon some Christian views of the material world. The theological circles I was raised in were careful to point out the value of both body and spirit. Yet, there was a strong preference for the spiritual realm over and above the material. This preference was mostly revealed in their view of the eternal state or end times. As I was taught, a season of time at the end would come in which the earth would be ruled

---

[8] Michael Horton, *The Christian Faith: A Systematic Theology for Pilgrims on the Way* (Grand Rapids, MI: Zondervan, 2011), 47.

[9] Gregg R. Allison, *Historical Theology* (Grand Rapids, MI: Zondervan 2011), 321-341.

physically by Jesus, but then the end would come and the physical realm would torched in God's judgment fire and all faithful Christians would be ushered to "heaven" where we would all have our individual clouds, harps, and wings and would sing forever.[10]

When it comes to talking about issues like the state of our environment, it was easy to believe that the material earth didn't matter and should not be cared for actively. I've been guilty of saying, "it's all going to burn anyway" failing to put biodegradable material into the recycle bin. In my mind, a theologically informed view of material place was ignored because I was a functional Platonist, believing that the spiritual concepts are what matter most.

Most of us probably don't even think about the philosophical underpinnings of this kind of worldview. We happen to be a bit more practical about life. We need places. I have to have a house to live in, an office to work at, and a park to take my children to play. Cities have to exist as population grows and people seek to efficiently work and live together. But we probably don't see the pizza place down the street as inherently valuable. Nor do we see the apartment complex we live in, the school buildings we attend, or the office spaces we work at as valuable.

---

[10] Millard J. Erickson's argument for the eternal state of the Christian seems to be more conceptual (rest, worship, service) than concrete. "Since God does not occupy space, which is a feature of our universe, it would seem that heaven is a state, a spiritual condition, rather than a place."

Millard J. Erickson, *Christian Theology* Second Edition, (Grand Rapids, MI: Baker Books, 1998), 1239.

For most of us, places are merely commodities that serve a purpose. Once a better place comes along that serves the perceived purpose in some way or another we reject the former place. Without realizing it, we become locational parasites that suck up resources and benefits of place, without giving a thought to replenishing or appreciating it. When the place becomes boring or "used up," we find a better place to go. Recently some friends of mine who lived in the same house in the same neighborhood for over a decade decided to move to a bigger, better house. They didn't necessarily need the new house they just liked it's location, the different school district, and local conveniences better than where they were at. So they uprooted all of their deeply built neighborhood relationships and relocated. Ten years of presence among non-Christian neighbors was finished, all for a better view out the window.

Think about the places around your city or town that are vacant or dilapidated right now. Why are they like that? Probably because more useful or functional places were conceived where the same purpose could be achieved, and the former place was discarded. Case in point: the strip mall. Once the predominate feature of American suburban cities in the 50's and 60's, they sought to replicate a downtown, store-front environment while making room for automobile parking. So why do so many strip malls look like garbage today? Because someone conceived of a better model, the shopping mall, where a large, multi-purpose structure was built with ample parking garages, movie theaters, and large department "anchor" stores. The strip mall was discarded for the shopping mall which is currently facing its own demise and is being replaced by. . . the boutique stores. Through this brief philosophical reflection, I hope you can see that our view of place matters.

Places Matter

We must deal with this quandary. Do physical places here and now matter? If we go back to the beginning of the Scripture story, we have to conclude that they do, mainly because God made a specific place.

Genesis 2 retells the creation story from another angle. In Genesis 1, we read of a universal creation. A creation of categories or "space." God makes heavens and earth, light and dark, sea and sky, land and ocean. All are categorical spaces in the universe. And he fills each space that he has formed. Inhabitants are brought into the spaces of sea, sky, land, and heavens.

Genesis 2 transports us to a specific place. God makes Eden. He cultivates the larger space of the earth he has made with specific boundaries, and creates "place." This place has named borders and geographic location markers, such as rivers. The space is filled with specific vegetation and distinct gems and minerals. Furthermore, God places specific inhabitants into this place with a specific function to carry out. Man and woman are placed here with the cultural mandate to cultivate and multiply. The Garden of Eden, this specific and named place, is theologically important. It is from this prototype of place (cultivated space filled with inhabitants for specific purposes) that every other place in the world derives itself. This Garden was not intended to stay an embryonic seedbed of existence but was intended to be multiplied, cultivated, and developed into larger places. The Garden was to become a city. This place was to be the first place from which all other places would take their cues to design culture, develop structure, and deploy a life lived in the presence of God.

Then the Fall happened.

The concept of place didn't fall apart altogether at the Fall. Places still mattered, and placed were still created. Cities were built and civilizations developed. Yet the key ingredient was missing in all of these. Eden was developed so that God and man could cohabitate together. The break in the Garden was a break in presence. Places continued to be created but instead of joyful interaction with God's presence these places became tributes to human independence from God. In fact, godless places proliferated.

Then the remedy came. The Son of God, Jesus was sent to live and inhabit our places. As the Son of God he embodied the presence of God among us (Jn. 1:14). In his incarnation, death, and resurrection he came to redeem both person and place (Col. 1:15-23) so that his name is "Immanuel", or God with us. (Matt. 1:18). Each and every place matters because God, in Christ, is with us.

We are however faced with another challenge because of this. Jesus is no longer in our places, on our planet. He has ascended back to heaven. It seems as if the break between God and man, spiritual and material is in effect and real once again. Maybe salvation really is just for the spiritual part of our being, more so than the physical part. If the fundamental theological definition for God is that he is "spirit" than maybe our physical lives, and physical places aren't all that important. Or maybe it is because we have failed to see how an ever-present God so wisely devised our redemption so that it would include both the spiritual and material so that , as Paul said, Christ would be "all, and in all" (Col. 3:17).

The everPresent God in Every Place

The challenge in viewing this division of material and spiritual centers around the question, how does a God who exists outside of time and space and place become localized in such a way that both people and place matter? To ask it another way, how does this enormous Creator-God shrink himself down to be fully real and fully present in the very teeny-tiny places of his creation? The answer is through his redeemed creation. He does it by redeeming people who live in these places.

On several occasions, I've been asked why God doesn't simply rapture people up to heaven as soon as they are saved. If we buy into the dualistic competition of spiritual and material then it would only seem logical for God to drop the material stuff as soon as possible so we could get on with the greater and better spiritual phase of our existence. However, if we believe that both physical and spiritual are important, integral parts of who we are as creatures then we need, by necessity, both spiritual and material restoration. This includes a renovation of the body and a renovation of places.

As Jesus relocates us from our rebellion and guilt into his family, he physically leaves us where we are. The moment I became a Christian, I wasn't transported to some ethereal space in an out-of-body way. I was still sitting in the back seat of my dad's station wagon. Now, the Jeremy sitting in the back of that station wagon is a different person. His identity isn't just "Jeremy Writebol." He is a new person (2 Cor. 5:17), who has a new identity (2 Pt. 2:9), and a new destiny. I became a child of God. As God's son I still inhabit a very specific and unique location, a place of flesh on a plot of land. Yet my relationship to those places has fundamentally changed.

Jesus' ascension back to the Father was so that he could send the Holy Spirit to indwell his people (Jn. 14:17). Now, in the back of that station wagon, God is present in the person of the Holy Spirit indwelling one of God's children. The God who is present everywhere is fully present everywhere in and through his people. This isn't limited to just one person in the back of one car on a cold night waiting for his mother to come out of the fabric store. Every person who has been reconciled to God through the work of Jesus is inhabited with the Holy Spirit wherever they are at. So the presence of God is everywhere God's people are.

Consider the fact that right now approximately seven billion people populate the planet. While it is difficult to state with firm accuracy it is estimated that there are some two billion Christians on the planet. That means that there are two billion places all over this earth where God's presence is embodied in his people. Two billion people that are indewlt by the Holy Spirit of God living in two billion places at two billion distinct moments. The God who exists above and outside of material time and place has fully located himself into time and space and place two billion times over in the very moment I type these words. His presence is a spiritual presence over the earth, but his presence is also a material presence living ordinary lives in ordinary places doing ordinary things. The God who is everywhere is also the God who is in every place through his people.

The King and His Kingdom

When Stephanie and I decided to move to Kansas one of the first things we began to work on was finding a place to live. The city was big and we wanted to be strategic and wise about where we would plant ourselves within the city. We had a list of preferences and priorities that would help us narrow down places that would be well suited for us to purchase a home. As we were thinking and pursuing our dream home in Kansas, one of the questions that we were constantly asking one another was "where *should* we live?" On one hand we knew we had the freedom to live anywhere in the city, but on the other hand we knew that where we located ourselves was going to be an important, even a strategic decision. We knew the gospel implications for where we lived were as deep as the gospel implications were for how we lived. As I was confessing this challenge to a new friend, he looked at me as if a deer was staring into headlights and said, "What does the gospel have to do with where you live? Just don't mess up how you live!" It was then that I realized that division of spiritual and material was so deep that it colored the way in which we see the gospel.

Maybe we struggle with this dichotomy of physical and spiritual so much because we struggle with the extent of the gospel itself. We believe that Jesus came and lived for us, died for us, and rose to life again so that we could have eternal life. This is all good and true, but what does it have to do with my everyday life here on planet Earth? What does the gospel have to do with where I walk, eat, drink, work, sleep, play, and so forth? What does it have to say about the places I inhabit?

Our problem is that we believe the gospel is a spiritual thing, but not so much a material thing. Yet, if we see that God creates and gives value to material things just as much as spiritual things, then wouldn't it make sense for the gospel to encompass both? If the gospel is more than spiritual truths about God, sinners, Jesus, and forgiveness but is a message of physical location, dislocation, and relocation, then there has to be a word of renovation to the broken places.

The reality of that gospel word is that it does include both material and spiritual realms. The simplest form of the gospel message in the Bible is "Jesus is Lord" (2 Cor. 4:5). However, that simple declaration is loaded with meaning. It is a declaration of a King, a sovereign who has authority over all people, places, rulers, and authorities (Eph. 1:20-21). It is the word of the One who has a Kingdom (Jn. 18:36). Yes, a kingdom that is not of this world, but a kingdom that is for and in and advancing in every place in this world (Matt. 24:14). That's why Jesus declared, "All authority in heaven and on earth has been given to me" (28:18). He is the King, and wherever the king is his kingdom is present.[11]

---

[11] Craig G. Bartholomew, *Where Mortals Dwell*, Baker Academic, 2011.

Relocation: How Christ Brings Exiled Children Home

Embassies are interesting locations to me. While they remain on the land of one nation, they are representative places of another nation. The Mexican embassy in the United States located in Washington D.C. is in some sense Mexico embodied in America. The representative of Mexico to the United States is the ambassador for the Mexican government to ours. In the same way, the gospel does this physically within our lives. Our homes, our workplaces, our social environments become little embassies of the King we represent, Christ. The kingdom of Christ is embodied in the physical places we inhabit. Furthermore we are designated as ambassadors of Christ into the surrounding places. As ambassadors we call people to be reconciled to God through Christ (2 Cor. 5:20). We declare the nature of the King and the values of his Kingdom. We call those who live in the kingdom of darkness to renounce that citizenship and be transferred into the kingdom of light by Christ (2 Pt. 2:9). This is fundamentally what we mean when we talk about the concept of mission.

The work of mission is the king's citizen-ambassadors, living in kingdom-embassies, taking the good news of the King ("Jesus is Lord") to all the places where that message is not believed and lived. Mission isn't so much about persuading someone to come over to your way of thinking on spiritual matters. Instead, mission is the work of calling dislocated people to reconciliation with the king and relocation into his Kingdom. Mission is done through the means of living under the authority Christ while declaring the kindness of Christ in every place that we inhabit. The extent of that mission is universal. Jesus' kingdom will encompass every place on this planet. His kingdom domain is a global kingdom. The worship of heaven in Revelation 5 assures us that people from every place on the globe will be reconciled by the blood of the Lamb (Rev. 5:9). Every place on the globe will be a kingdom place because every place will be renovated to be a reflection in word and in deed of the Kingdom of God. This is why place is so important. The kingdom belongs everywhere.

Renovation in the Kingdom

Places matter because the King is present. And the reign of the King in the lives of his people in this world, in their places, means that the Kingdom should be reflected. As Craig Bartholomew states, "Just as the presence of the Holy One among the Israelites was to permeate every aspect of their lives, so now this is how it is to be throughout the creation, as groups of followers live the life of the kingdom in their particular places."[12]

To be an American means to have certain traits that are quintessentially "American." When you travel to other places, your traits don't change. For instance, Americans have a reputation for being loud in other cultures. It's who we are. Our British friends are known for being reserved, sarcastic and cynical about everything. The Australians are off-the-hook crazy, crocodile-wrestling, "another shrimp on the barbie" fanatics (or at least the ones I've seen on television). Each of us have our own cultural traits that reveal our native locations.

---

[12] Bartholomew, 117.

So it is with the Kingdom of God. As God's people are indwelt with God's presence, we are sent out to live under the authority of the King, reflecting his reign in every aspect of our lives. We want to show the world what the Kingdom of God is like.

As all things are being made new, so it is with our places. They are transformed from just boxes with walls to real places where we live transformed lives under the authority of the king. Places become outposts of the Kingdom.

Imagine what a place would be like if Kingdom citizens, living under the authority of the King, were living in the presence of the King. This is what it means for God to be with us. We are pursuing a life of the Kingdom. It won't be a perfect life; it won't be a life that fully realizes the transformation that the King brings about. It will be a life of tension, living in the already of being in the kingdom that has not yet been fully realized. And yet, through little glimmers and acts and deeds, the places we live will begin to more clearly reflect the renovation of the King.

Renovation of Real Places

There is a building in the downtown area of Seattle that has a notorious history. The Tabella Restaurant and Lounge was once the epicenter of violence, drugs, and sexual dysfunction. Police were often called to the club to handle violent activity. Cages for housing go-go dancers lined the walls of the room. The abuse of drugs, alcohol, and sex there led to destroyed lives. Did this place matter?

For those who hold to a mere spiritual emphasis of the gospel, it wouldn't matter. Let it burn. But if the gospel is a declaration of the King who makes all things new, then that has to include a place as notorious as The Tabella. The King's gracious reign must renovate a place of evil and brokenness to a place that reflects the values of the Kingdom.

Places matter. And when a church in Seattle bought and renovated the building so that they could gather weekly to worship in that space, they left one of the go-go cages standing. That cage was a reminder of what that place was, and its function was altered so that the message of the King could be broadcast to the greater world. As the people of space and place are changed by the grace of God, so also do their places change because of the grace of God.[13]

Now every place matters because the King is everywhere through His people. Now every place matters because the Kingdom is coming to bear. One day, all things will be made new.

---

[13] This story was documented at the website, http://www.seattlepi.com/local/article/Mars-Hill-Church-opens-in-ex-Tabella-nightclub-1267374.php. Accessed 12.31.13

Questions for Group Discussion:
1. Where have you seen a renovation project take place before? What did it entail? How was the project better when it was finished?
2. In what ways has the division between material and spiritual been evident in your thinking and life? How has this chapter challenged those viewpoints?
3. How does the metaphor of a king and his kingdom impact the way you see the transformation of the places you live in today?
4. How does the imagery of an embassy and ambassador help you understand mission and renovation today?

Part 2: The everPresent Gospel in Everyday Life

As a pastor, I hold a several key convictions about how theology works. First, I believe in the work of theology. I believe theology must be *thoughtful*, reflective. It is essential to study God in order to know him. If we do not know God rightly, we cannot live the Christian life rightly. So the study of God is of supreme importance. However, theology by itself has to have an orientation. My second conviction is that theology must become *practical* or, as older theologians called it, experiential. Theology must work. It must be lived out in the real everyday world. Finally, theology must be *missional*. It must work, not only for ourselves but also for others. Since the Scripture-story is a story of God's mission to "seek and save the lost" (Lk. 19:10), our unpacking of theology must also possess an outward trajectory to relocate a dislocated world. These convictions undergird this entire book and play out more specifically in this second section. As we build a theology of place, we must see how that theology translates into our practice and God's mission within specific, everyday places.

Sociology has done a helpful job of defining specific categories of place that most of us weave in and out of every day. Books like Ray Oldenburg's *The Great Good Place* have helped define the concept of the "Third Place" that businesses such as Starbucks have adapted for their stores to create places in which community life is fostered and developed. It's my intention in this section to examine the way an ever-present gospel comes to bear on everyday life within the realm of four categorized places: home, work, social environments, and city. In this section we will move from the smallest and most intimate expression of place, the home, to the largest unifying description of place, the city with stops at intermediate places along the way.

Chapter 5
The everPresent Gospel in First Places: The Home

At this very moment, my home is a bakery as well as a recreational center and office. My wife is upstairs in the kitchen, baking hundreds of cupcakes for a school event tonight. The gingerbread and espresso scents move throughout the rooms of the house. I see an expert at work. My children are at rest. Sitting on the couch watching Saturday morning cartoons, they laugh and giggle at the slap-stick comedy of talking animals. They wrestle and argue with each other over what show they will get to watch next or what game they will play. And I am in the basement of our house, sitting at my personal bar-turned-desk, surrounded by papers and books, Waves of indie-rock float over me as I write in between sips of dark coffee. Our home, for the moment, is a place of harmony, industry, and relaxation.

The house itself is a 1920's two-story with three bedrooms, one and a half baths, a spacious dining room and family room, and a partially renovated basement. There is a detached garage that leans a bit to the east from age and a fenced backyard covered in the leaves that fell this autumn from the trees surrounding our house. When we moved from California to Kansas, we ran across this house on the Internet and initially dismissed it, but through a funny act of Providence, we ended up buying it. Much has changed in terms of style and culture both inside and outside this house since we took possession of it (namely the removal of the "Boomer Sooner" doorbell). Nevertheless, this place is still a home on Woodrow and it has been for almost one-hundred years now. So what does the presence of God have to do with a place like this? What does an ever-present gospel tell me about my home, how I should live in it, what colors I should paint it, and what function it should have in my daily life? How does a theology of space and place come to bear at home?

What Makes A Place?

Before we push into practical aspects of how to apply an ever-present gospel to the sphere of our everyday places, perhaps we should lie out a specific paradigm of what place is.

As I mentioned earlier, Eden was the prototype of the concept of place. As the first place, it contained everything that would grow and flourish into the places we move in and around each and every day. Looking at Eden we see a clear description of a distinct place being a cultivated space filled with inhabitants for specific purposes. Furthermore, gospel-shaped places are those that are actively engaged by the real presence of Christ as King within them. Let me unpack briefly what I mean by this.

First, place is *cultivated*. It's not open, undesignated, undeveloped area. To say it another way, place has design. The architects of our buildings, cities, and even our homes have an important role in shaping not only the function of the place, but also descriptively cultivating the shape of that place so it's design and function work together. God, as the greatest Architect, has uniquely designed each place in this universe to artistically achieve the function for which he created each place.

Second, place has a *function*. These functions can be diverse and unique, but for a place to be a place and not just some area of the universe far and wide, it has to have a specific role it plays in that universe. A home is different from an office building. Office buildings are different from city parks or restaurants or shopping malls. Each place has a specific role to play with the design it takes and the inhabitants that occupy that space.

Third, place has *inhabitants*. There have to be beings that dwell within a place for it to be "somewhere." Think about why they call wilderness places "the middle of nowhere." It's often because there is nobody in that place. Even the region of the solar system above the atmosphere of planet Earth is designated "outer space" because, at least as far as limited humanity can tell, there aren't too many inhabitants out there. Place is real because it has people within it.

A final, distinguishing feature of a gospel-shaped place is that the reality of Christ as Lord is felt and lived within that space. Every space inhabited by people who live under the kingship of Christ is a dwelling in the domain of the Kingdom. These newly renovated Kingdom places are inhabited by the King himself through his Spirit-inhabited people. So the life of the Kingdom of God is seen through the innumerable Kingdom outposts occupied by Kingdom citizens. From this the world sees the greatness, grace, and glory of the King and his Kingdom. The world is invited to confess their dislocation, repent, and return home only through Jesus and begin the renovation of their places as Kingdom outposts. These places still have cultivated design, function, and inhabitants but they now have a new and greater reality, namely God's presence.

In that light, we can walk into each place that we live, seeking to apply the specific layers of a place. The gospel, being a total and complete reorientation of our lives under the kingly authority of the crucified, risen Jesus, comes to bear on the cultivated designs, inhabitants, and functions of the places we engage every day.

So what does this have to do with our first places, our homes?

Homemaking: A Blueprint for The Kingdom Home

Noah and Anna are unique. They have five children ranging in age from twelve to two. At a clip of every two years another child came into their home. Stephanie and I are a bit different, but maybe more common. We have two children. Both are young but there was a gap of three years between our two. Josh and Christine have two children as well. Biologically they were not able to have their own children, but from the moment Grace and Owen were born, they were in the arms of their adoptive parents. Ed and Debbie gave birth to three children; however, each one was eight years old when the next came along.

By the time their oldest child was eighteen, she had a ten-year-old and a two-year-old brother.

Each family situation is unique, just as each house as a place is unique. I have yet to find two homes that share the exact same stories, cultures, and designs. Even if the exteriors of prefabricated model homes are the same, the interiors demonstrate a difference in styles, personal preferences, and tastes. The distinct nature and culture of a house takes an entirely different scale when it's examined on a global scale. Those who live on the Amazon River under a thatched roof have a different concept of a house than those who live in suburban single-family homes. Even high-density homes in the cities of Japan are distinct from the flats of metropolitan Moscow. A house is as different as the world in which it was formed. One friend tells me that some Haitians consider Americans "box people" because all we do is exist in box-like structures.

Yet these places, as different as they are and as multi-faceted as their distinctions, share a common point of reference. While the shape, size, and look of a house are distinct from place to place, every house on earth shares an inherent feature. The house is the living space of the family. Home is where societal life is conceived, cultivated, and multiplied at the smallest level. This is the blueprint of the Kingdom home. A place where citizens of the kingdom make, mature, and multiply kingdom citizens.

Homes are places where Kingdom citizens are to conceive, care for, train, and then send mature Kingdom citizens who will marry, conceive, care for, train, and then send mature Kingdom citizens who will advance the Kingdom to the next generation.

Making a Home Means Making Babies

Let's look again briefly at the home in the Scriptures and, specifically, the prototypical home in Eden. Eden was a place of defined boundary and location. In it were placed two inhabitants, Adam and Eve (Gen. 2:7). The function of their first home, Eden, was to be a place of safety, provision, and development. They found safety within Eden because of its boundaries and the protective role those boundaries played with regard to the outside world. They found provision in that every tree within the Garden was given by God to physically sustain them (1:29). They also found that the Garden was given as a place for development. Their mandate, or role, within that first home was to cultivate the garden and multiply their family (1:28, 2:15). They were to shape the design and context of their home as well as growing their family within the context of the home. God's presence with them was as Creator and King and this home was the beachhead of his growing and advancing universal Kingdom.

Their first mandate wasn't to be mainly gardeners. The first mandate of humanity was to be procreative. Dominion over everything would be a second dimension of their mandate but initially God called forth humanity to reproduce and "be fruitful." The Kingdom home, first and foremost, is for the population of a Kingdom.

This stands in the face of current cultural trends regarding children and the life of the home. Recently *Time Magazine* celebrated the life of young, affluent married couples who were "childfree."[14] To these couples, children are seen as a hindrance to achieving their career goals or the luxury lifestyle they wish to achieve. Furthermore, there is a large sense of disdain and mockery for those with larger families.[15] Our culture wants all of the pleasure of sexuality but none of the responsibility that comes with sexuality.

Yet the home is the place for sex. It's the place where a married man and woman enjoy the safety of being naked without shame. It's the place where intimacy in marriage is cultivated and then multiplied in the form of conceived children. The home is the place where Kingdom citizens fulfill the mandate to cultivate a new generation of loyal followers of the King. By implication this means that, *as God allows,* every Christian should endeavor to get married and have children. Making a home for the Kingdom means, at the most basic level, fulfilling the mandate to make babies. This does not mean that every Christian will be married and have children, but again, *as God allows,* this should be the default intention of our home lives. More will be said later for those who do not experience these realities currently.

Cultivating Kingdom Citizens

The home, however, is for more than just reproduction. The home is also a training ground. As every act of

---

[14] "The Childfree Life," *Time Magazine,* August 12, 2013.

[15] San Diego Chargers quarterback Philip Rivers is commonly attacked for having six children.
http://espn.go.com/nfl/story/_/id/9540219/san-diego-chargers-qb-philip-rivers-answers-fans-questions-espn-magazine. **Accessed 12.31.13**

God's creation came with responsibility to cultivate that creation, so every act of procreation comes with the responsibility of cultivating those new lives. In homes where the gospel is ever-present, children aren't merely conceived; they are cultivated as Kingdom citizens.

One night I came home to find that my son's car seat was sitting in the kitchen with all the fabric covering removed. Stephanie was attempting to clean the filth off of a well-traveled car seat and wanted to give it the proper cleansing it needed. Because a car seat without any of its covering except the foam protectors can be an attractive toy to curious children, she told my daughter not to play with the car seat. Replacing the seat was an expensive proposition that we didn't really want to undertake. As you might expect, curiosity (and a large measure of disobedience) got the better of my daughter. As she played around with the car seat, and specifically the expensive foam braces on the car seat, we heard the distinct sound of the popping of foam. And then she ran. Upon inspection, we discovered the very parts of the car seat that we were concerned with her breaking were the exact ones that she had broken. Now judgment was upon our disobedient daughter Allison. After we sent her to her room, Stephanie and I tried to figure out what we should do. I had no clue, but I knew that in front of us stood a moment to cultivate a kingdom home. Allison had disobeyed the word of her mother, she had broken the very thing we told her not to play with, and she had no way to pay for it.

I went back to her room to talk with her and figure out a punishment and I told her the car seat was very expensive. As awkward as it was, I shared that she should probably give up the money that she had saved from Christmas to pay for the car seat. When I said that to her, she broke into tears. But it wasn't because she faced the prospect of losing all her saved money. The problem for Allison was that she didn't have enough to pay for it. She lacked the ability to properly repay the debt she had incurred.

In that moment, the Holy Spirit reminded me of a dislocating debt I had incurred with nowhere near the sufficient amount of funds to repay it. I'm far from a perfect parent and most days probably struggle to rate as even a good one, but I had a moment to cultivate an ever-present gospel within my daughter.

With tears running down my cheeks, I told her that I had owed a debt I couldn't pay and that Jesus had paid it for me so that I could be free. And with joy I told my daughter I had enough to cover the entire cost of the broken car seat so that she could be free of the debt she owed to me. It was a simple example but cultivating a kingdom home means building the gospel story into the lives of our children. It also reminds us of the gospel we as parents need so desperately.

Cultivating kingdom citizens means training them in the way they should go (Prov. 22:6). It means showing them the Law of God and then the grace of the gospel. It means dealing with their sinful heart more than their sinful behavior by pointing them to the only one who can change their heart. It's constantly, proactively, demonstratively sharing the way of the Kingdom with our children. Cultivating an ever-present Gospel in our homes means reading the Bible with our children (Deut. 6:7), sharing Jesus with our children, and demonstrating the unconditional, identifying love of God the Father to our children as human fathers and mothers (Lk. 11:1-13). It means showing our children and others the realities of God's adoption of us into his family by the way we adopt the needy and fatherless into our families (Eph. 1:5).

Cultivation requires work. It requires intentionality. It requires patience. Just as seeds in a garden take water, fertilized soil, and lots of time, so our children need environments of the gospel to grow and develop into relocated, fruit-bearing citizens of the Kingdom of God. It requires the grace and presence of God to bring the children we conceive who are in darkness into the marvelous light of Christ (1 Pt. 2:9). We will cultivate a house for God by the way we are present with the gospel in our children's lives.

From One Family to a Multitude of Families

Yet a home isn't just a place to make and train children. The kingdom home is a launching pad. When we read Genesis 1 and think about the cultural mandate to be fruitful and multiply, we often think of it as a command to increase the earth's population. If that were the case, then any sort of sexual ethic would have to be tossed out the window as long as babies were made. But the cultural mandate has a specific context to be fulfilled in. To God, the means are just as important as the end. The means for filling the earth is within the context of the home. Sexuality's right context is that of a married man and a married woman who embrace the reality that through their union they will be multiplying their home. The cultural mandate wasn't just to make babies; it was to make and multiply homes.

I dread the day my daughter introduces me to "the one." I dread the day that he comes to my home, sits down with me, and proceeds to ask me for her hand in marriage. And yet I only dread that day because of how much I love my little girl. I'm a jealous dad that doesn't want other boys stealing her affections. Still as I think about the purpose of my home and the sense of an ever-present gospel applied to it, I get excited about that day. It excites me because I see a greater story at work. I see something far greater than just legacy or a name for myself down the line. I see the multiplication of homes for the sake of the King. Instead of there being just one household worshipping Jesus, the fruit of my witness and work as a father, by God's grace, extends beyond me to my children and grandchildren. This could be true of every family.

The goal of conceiving and cultivating children isn't just to have well-adjusted adults who won't make a larger mess when they enter the world. The goal of the gospel-shaped home is the sending of our children to live in their homes and bear witness to the relocating power of Jesus as King over all kings. This is often the reason the Scriptures describe the church as a household (Eph. 2:19). In the same way the church is called to make disciples, develop, and then deploy them, the home is a first place for the making of disciples, developing, and then deploying them. The missionary strategy of the church is first played out in the home itself.

Consider the reason we call genealogies a "family tree." The branches of the tree are intended to spread out, rise up, and flourish beyond the initial trunk of the tree from which they come. At least on my street, the larger trees are the more beautiful ones particularly because of how high they reach and how strong they are. So it is with kingdom families. As Christ has come to reclaim our lives, he completely renovates our concepts of family and transforms them into living households of his that are growing in size, strength, reach, and potential for the reclaiming and renovating of new homes for his sake. The mustard seed of the house is the environment through which the kingdom of God advances day to day to day as we live with present intentionality in our homes.

Renovating Broken Homes

As ideal as all this sounds – get married, make babies, train and teach them the gospel, and then send them to get married, make babies and so forth – there is the stark reality of our fallenness and dislocation. So many homes are broken, so many children are fatherless, and the very meaning of family and house distorted, sometimes beyond recognition.

For some couples reading this chapter, having children is a heartfelt desire but, for various reasons, God has not allowed that to be the case. For others, they have sought to be a home in which the gospel is cultivated and a kingdom outpost that would deploy a multiplying force of children for Jesus' sake. For various reasons as well, these ambitions have not been realized. These are painful issues which can bring about guilt, shame, and a further sense of dislocation from God's original design.

The story isn't fully told however. As long as we have life and breath and are awake to live out another day, the gospel still bears impact on our homes, whatever their state. The relocating, renovating work of Jesus is still active, forming the household of God.

More than anything it should be realized that Christ is the one who calls us into his household. Having children, raising them to love Jesus, and then sending them in marriage to have children, raise them to love Jesus, and send them out does not justify us. Any attempts at relocating ourselves back into Christ through our own efforts of renovation are merely religious forms that we use to glorify ourselves. Not a single family will stand before the Lord accepted into his family because they had a good marriage and three children who grew up and were responsible contributors to society who had three children who did the same. We will be accepted because of what Christ has done. Nothing less than that and certainly nothing more. So as the dislocating realities of our world bring barrenness and brokenness within our families, our identity as kingdom citizens remains intact, even if our efforts to build a gospel-formed household do not.

The good news of the gospel is that anyone can be part of the household of God, and anyone can begin, by God's grace, to live presently in their household as a citizen of the kingdom. The work of renovation begins today as we seek to apply this relocating, renovating message to our homes by living for the kingdom here and now in our first places, our homes.

Questions for Group Discussion:

1. How is Eden the prototypical place? What does it show us about what purposes and functions created places are to have?
2. What is the primary purpose of the home? Who is to inhabit the home? How should it be cultivated?
3. How do kingdom homes demonstrate the presence of God in their midst? How do they advance the gospel?
4. What good news is there for broken homes? How is the gospel applied here?

Chapter 6
The everPresent Gospel in
Second Places: The Office

Eric sat across the table enjoying a slice of pizza with me. His face told me all I needed to know about his day so far. Facing a pretty heavy deadline, and apparently limited resources to meet the deadline, I could tell his job wasn't as fun as I dreamed it might be. He confessed to me that working each day designing personal jets and luxury airliners wasn't as important, in his mind, as my work of pastoring a church and making disciples. In Eric's mind, the task of aeronautical engineering paid the bills, but it wasn't fulfilling a life passion or a greater aim of doing things that would last for eternity. He was just managing a team of employees to design and develop airplanes.

Bonnie spends close to eighty hours a week as a medical resident at a local hospital. After finishing medical school with her husband Brandon, they moved on to residency and have been working to help people in every department from trauma to sports medicine. While they feel good about being able to help people, they both have shared the emotional drain of not seeing patients get better. Their desire to see progress made in the long-term and overall health of the people they serve is often thwarted by addictive dependencies and behavioral tendencies. The frustration of rarely seeing progress mounts on them daily.

Andy struggled with what he was going to do to make ends meet for his family. Although he never finished college, he enjoyed learning and found several jobs that employed him well. Managing the material supplies and resources of the law offices of the local county government provided him with a good income and steady hours. But that wasn't where Andy wanted to spend his life working; he wanted to serve the city in a more tangible way. So he enrolled in the police academy where he finished second in his class and was hired by the county sheriff's office as a deputy. Unfortunately, during his initial test phase, he was overcome by the stress of the job and ended up transitioning to answering 9-1-1 calls as a dispatcher. It was a season of disappointment and frustration as the dream he pursued seemed just beyond his grasp. Work for Andy was merely a means to pay the bills, even if it wasn't what he really wanted to do.

These are stories of people I know who struggle with their work. Pretty much everybody I can think of wrestles with either the productivity or apparent futility of their job. Nobody I know, on most days, loves what they routinely do. Yet it has to get done. For the greater part of our waking lives, we exist as people at work. The "office" as a place is a familiar, routine, and even loathed environment that causes us to wonder why so much of our lives are spent in futility at work. Does the gospel have anything to say about the where and the why of our work?

If we believe that the gospel is the word of a Savior-King who relocates us from death into his kingdom which is being unveiled even in the here and now, then the King has much to say about our work. This ever-present gospel presents for us a way of life at our offices and workplaces that demonstrates both the authority of the King as well as the nature of the Kingdom. The way in which we work shows the world a productive, effective King that uses all things, even bread-making and banking, to bring glory to himself as the King of all Kings.

Work Is Right

One of the common misconceptions we as humans make about the nature of work is that work is part of the curse. The belief on the street is that work was non-existent until Adam and Eve took that fatal bite. As a measure to keep humanity under his boot, God invented the particular curse of manual labor and a working human society. But that idea ignores the larger scope of the Scripture story, namely that God is a working God who created a working people. The creation week itself demonstrates God as a working-class God who is speaking and creating, forming and filling. The Creator spent six days laboring and one day resting from his work.

Furthermore, since God made humanity in his image, he gave to them a place to work and develop. The second part of the cultural mandate found in Genesis 1 was that humanity wasn't just to make families but they were to develop, maintain, cultivate, and exercise authority over the whole of creation (Gen. 1:28). Anytime I go out in my backyard and try to develop, maintain, cultivate, and exercise authority over it, I am working. Work is essential to the human role.

This is why we must see that the curse wasn't that humanity would be workers. Being someone who works is part of our created structure. It is a role we've been given to play in the theater of God. Work is a glorious thing, mainly because it displays a working God. When we labor to create, manufacture, develop, and cultivate the elements of this world in some fashion or another, we are demonstrating God-at-the-office. He of course made the universe his office and then went to work in it. The office, classroom, retail store, restaurant, factory, and laboratory are all places in which created humanity exercises dominion to cultivate and develop God's initial creation. Work is essential to who we are. Work is right.

Work builds strong economic systems in which resources are shared and people are provided for. Work develops culture (otherwise known as technology) and enhances means by which God's glory is seen. Work provides structure and importance to our day-to-day lives by giving us a way to contribute to the greater good in the world. Work develops the skill, wisdom and craftsmanship of those who are laboring to demonstrate the skill, wisdom and craftsmanship of God. Even Jesus' occupation as a carpenter is a helpful example for us of the nature of working a job. He was a skilled craftsman in building, designing and forming furniture and structures. By the fact that he worked a job he shows us the essential nature of work in our daily lives.

There are times when you can tell that someone actually does enjoy their work. You see it in the expressed detail of the things they are working on. Randy, another friend of mine, has been working on a super-secret project at his business for the last two years. I am sure there were times when the work felt like a curse and he had to navigate through the complexities of management, deadlines, and long hours. Going into the office was anything but a delight. Yet the text messages I received from Randy on the day the new fighter jet he had been engineering was made public indicated exactly the opposite. He loved his work. He found it fulfilling to see a project come to completion. He was so excited to be at the office. Why? Because he was fulfilling part of what God had made him to display. Work.

A Bad Day at the Office

So why is it that we so deeply despise going to work? What is it about the office that causes us to prefer calling in sick, staying in bed, or hiding out for months on end rather than be doing the very thing that God called us to do with his good creation in the first place? Maybe going into the office really was the curse of our dislocation. It seems that work really was the result of our crimes.

Scripture makes it plain in Genesis 2 that work was given to humanity and work was right. But instead of work as we know it, work initially was not about providing for our essential needs like food and shelter. For our first parents, work was art. It was labor to design, cultivate, and express dominion over the established place of God. It was an effort to put decorations and details on the first place of God.

Occasionally, there are projects that I get to spend time working on that are sheer pleasure. They do not provide food for my table or pay off the mortgage. Instead they are labors of love. Tonight my daughter interrupted my writing and asked me to assemble her new LEGO stables. Some 2,000 pieces (and many of them very tiny) and two hours later, we were done. It wasn't anything I was paid to do, but it was still work. And I loved it. This is what going to the office was originally about: forming, cultivating, and managing creatively what God had made. It was art.

Then came the dislocating break of our rebellion. We didn't want to be artists painting on God's canvas. We wanted to make our own canvas. With it came the curse that now plagues our work. Instead of having everything we needed for life, we had to labor to stay alive. Where we were once amply supplied by God, now we were forced to have our cake and eat it, too. We wanted to work independently from God and he allowed it. We have to work to stay alive. This is the daily reality of our rebellion and the curse.

The office lost all of its delight. We found productivity flittered away by thorns and thistles. The soil we needed to survive was dry, hard, and unyielding. Making an existence from day-to-day, paycheck-to-paycheck became our work, and that was where work lost all its art.

Maybe this is why no one feels like going to work in the morning. Mondays are synonymous with the death of our freedom, independence, and life. Work is death and no one likes it. We spend our youth preparing to work, our best years working away, and then end up dying from our work. As the preacher of Ecclesiastes wonders, "What does man gain by all the toil at which he toils under the sun?" (Ecc. 1:3). This is the blatant effect of our sin and the curse. The office is a den of death.

This is why my friends Bonnie and Brandon don't see the progress of patients recovering to complete health. It's the reason why the hours and hours Eric spends designing aircraft feel fruitless. It's why Andy works a job he doesn't really desire so that he can put food on the table. It is why, although we seem to see developments in technology, science, politics, economics and the like, nothing seems to be getting better.

Work as Role or Identity?

Is there redemption for our offices? Although we believe in a gospel that saves our souls, could we imagine Christ redeeming our workplaces as well? Could there be salvation for the office too? Yes, but only if we look to the work of Christ. For so many, our work has transitioned itself from a role we were given to an identity we possess. Work became who we are instead of something we do.

The proof of this is found when you meet someone new. Introduce yourself to someone you don't know and the likelihood of you identifying yourself by what you do is very high. Usually we start with our name ("I'm Jeremy") followed by what we do ("I'm a pastor"). We weigh the value of our lives by our work. The important people are the ones with the great jobs, the large incomes, the high-yield, high-capacity productions. Those who achieve their vocational dreams are the great ones. Those who fail at attaining those degrees are just "working for the man."

We live and die by our jobs and their perceived successes and failures.

That's why we need a relocation. Our identity must be shifted away from what we do to who we are. We must be redeemed from perverting our role as workers into our identity as workers.

I find it wonderful that Jesus didn't come with an identity-issue about his work. He knew who he was, the Son of God. He knew what his job was, to give his life as a ransom for many (Mk. 10:45). He didn't have the two confused. And so he came, reminded of his identity by his Father (1:11) to do the work he was sent to do (1:15). He came to do the work we could not do. In substituting himself for us, he worked to fulfilled the Law at every point and win perfect righteousness for us. By standing in our place, he did the work of satisfying God's wrath and removing our sin by dying on the cross for us. In such, he glorified his father and accomplished the work he was sent to do (Jn. 17:5).

Jesus didn't take work away from us. He redeemed us from a life of finding our identity in our work. He didn't live, die, and rise to life again so that we could skip out on the office or marketplace. He lived, died, and arose to life again so that we would glorify him at our office, not worship our office. Instead of living to fulfill the identities we find in our work, Jesus gives us a new identity, his brothers and sisters, so that we can go to work, not to earn an identity but to rest from identity seeking. We go into the office as kingdom citizens to create, cultivate, develop, and design all that the King owns for the King's glory.

Who Are You Working For?

One of the most frustrating aspects of work, beyond the inefficiencies and futility of fruitless work, is the people we work for. Just as we struggle with deep authority issues in relationship with God, we continue to struggle with the authority issues we have with our employers and supervisors. Our bosses can be tyrants, ogres, and despots all in one eight-hour shift. For those of us who are fortunate enough to have a decent boss, we still buckle, from time to time, under the difficulty of not always seeing eye-to-eye. We all have bad days with our superiors.

For Kingdom citizens, the presence of the King in our workplaces deeply alters the way we see our bosses. Paul calls Kingdom citizens to see their work in this light by calling servants to be obedient and submissive to their superiors as if they were serving the King himself (Col. 3:22-24). The renovated heart goes beyond just obedience as a people-pleaser, or giving appearance as such, and calls the citizens of the Kingdom to obey with sincerity while fearing the Lord.

My fighter-jet-engineering friend Randy told me one day of a meeting with his superiors. In the meeting over the design of the jet, his boss became rather irate and excessively direct about a particular portion of the jet's design. Randy was given clear directions that the design of the jet should in every way be "from scratch." It was as if his company wanted to be the Wright brothers all over again and invent flight, this time on the scale of a fighter jet. As Randy debated for particular design similarities, his boss became more and more indignant about the uniqueness of the design. As Randy listened and considered, he knew that he had a responsibility to obey his boss and honor Christ. It didn't make sense, but it was right. It was only later that he discovered his boss's reasons and Randy ended up benefiting his company and business by his obedience.

This is the kind of renovating work the King does. He transforms his people from rebellious people-pleasers to sincere Kingdom-servants. Work is transformed by the way we work for the ones set in authority over us (1 Pt. 2:13-25).

Working Hard, Working Well

While obedience to our superiors is a kingdom value, is this all that a renovation of our work places brings about? Are we to just be dutiful drones at the jobs in which we take no delight? Does the gospel speak to what we spend our working lives doing? Is there a Kingdom renovation to be done with regard to occupations and vocations? Can a kingdom citizen find the art in their work once again?

Like the false dichotomy of the material and spiritual, bad religion created another dichotomy with regard to our work; sacred and secular. Those that worked jobs in the sacred realms of the church were the ones who worked within a higher calling. They had the blessing of God, treasure in heaven, and a trophy of accomplishing something that lasts for eternity to put on their mantle. For the bankers, butchers, and builders (also known as secular workers), there was the glib promise that one day they could go to heaven and maybe be a worship leader and really please God. However, their vocations and their work were sub-eternal and a less than great calling. What does God need with someone who can carve meat anyway? To this day, it's not too hard to find churches and Christians who still practically affirm this position.

But the Scriptures never affirm a sacred/secular vocational divide. Rather, the word of the King is that "*whatever you do*, work heartily, as for the Lord" (Col 3:23). Those three words, "whatever you do," are a major blow to any scared/secular mentality. In those words, the King affirms the unique occupations of Kingdom citizens. Whether it's banking, broadcasting, auto sales, brewing coffee, serving tables, or working at homemaking, the King authorizes his citizens to work well in what they do. He affirms the value of every occupation that cultivates, develops, and advances his authority in his Kingdom. This includes building bridges, teaching children, accounting financial assets, diagnosing physical diseases, and baking pies.

How is this so? How does the bakery become a Kingdom place? First, by the way in which we work. Paul says "whatever you do, do it heartily." There is a way in which Kingdom citizens work for the King. They, by their presence at their work, demonstrate God's nature. They reveal the God who worked hard at the creating of all things; a God who put his full wisdom and glory and creativity into play as he made all things. By the way they work, they show an industrious, productive, intelligent God. They show a God who didn't take short-cuts, who didn't get lazy on the job, and who didn't "phone it in" in his work of creation and redemption.

Second, they also show a Kingdom value in the trajectory of their work. They work "as for the Lord." Their work is aimed at pleasing the King himself. How does an aerospace engineer design planes for the Lord? By making the best planes he can. By using the wisdom and understanding and knowledge the King has gifted him with to understand the laws of nature and develop means by which the creation can be advanced to serve people. How does a baker make pies for the Lord? By baking in such a way that the King himself would enjoy her pies. By baking with a mind to serve her fellow humanity as they delight in the excellent tastes of the pie. They both please the Lord by being creative, honest, diligent, and excellent in their various occupations.

There is a further implication of the resurrection of Jesus here for us in our work. The resurrection of Jesus was his coronation and enthronement as King over all kings. Everything is being brought under subjection to him as King (Ps. 8:6, 1 Cor. 15:27). Our work, done in the name of the King and for the King is participating with him in bringing all things under his authority. The way we develop technology, or manage resources, or develop business strategies, or cook meals, or build houses, or any innumerable sorts of occupations are bringing all things under subjection to Christ. The computer programmer who develops software to advance communication can see himself as utilizing technology for the sake of the King and the advancement of his Kingdom. The doctor who develops wise and resourceful medical practices is bringing the field of medicine under the realm of the King when she does so to keep, preserve and enhance life. The teacher who works with fourth graders is bringing a classroom of students under the dominion of Christ, but educating her class about the physical and moral laws that govern the world in which we live in. All things are brought to rest under the Lordship of Christ as the resurrected King.

As such, the renovating work of the King brings us to our offices (or classrooms or kitchens or laboratories, or whatever we call the space we work in) to work hard and to work for him. He calls us into every sphere of life and vocation to develop and deploy our gifts to show His authority and dominion over all things. He must have workers in every vocation to demonstrate all things are for his glory, even the offices that we spend our days working in. By our work we display an ever-present King in every place.

Questions for Group Discussion:
1. Why do we find work so difficult and unfulfilling?
2. How are our workplaces and offices renovated to be places for the King and his Kingdom?
3. What attitudes and behaviors should inform the way we work for non-Christian employers?
4. How can work be a source of joy to us even when we find it a burden or difficult?

Chapter 7
The everPresent Gospel in Third Places: Social Environments

Where do you like to hang out? Apart from your home where you eat and sleep and apart from your workplace where you spend your days making a living, where do you go to hang out? What places do you like to visit to enjoy the company of others, build relationships, and relax together?

For me, this place is a coffee shop that recently opened in downtown Wichita. One reason is because it offers the best coffee in town (this from a self-admitted "coffee snob"), but it's also a place where I feel at home. I regularly meet with people at the coffee shop and try to go there almost daily. The owners are some of the friendliest people I know. The shop itself sits on the corner of one of the major streets in town, so it's always a vibrant place to watch people and traffic go by. But this place is more than just a commercial box designed to dispense coffee. For me it has more value than just great coffee.

This coffee shop is where some of the best conversations I've had have taken place. It is where Stephanie and I have seen new relationships kindled and developed.

I have experienced grace and kindness in unique ways
here. People that I would not normally get to know because of where I live and work are now frequent connec-
tions in my life because of this little coffee shop. An inter-
connected web of relationships that are as vast and diverse as our city has developed, all from within a place
that sits on the corner of Douglas and St. Francis. A community has arisen from a third place.

Where Are the Third Places?

American "third places" are a bit vague and difficult
to understand. For most of the world, having a pub or city
plaza to meet with people, share life, and recreate within
is a standard design of a city. Sociologist like James How-
ard Kunstler have bemoaned the fact that America doesn't
understand the need for these sorts of environments.[16]
Others, such as Ray Oldenburg, have coined the term the
"Third Place" and identified the need for socially valuable
places like coffee shops, bars, hair salons, and bookstores.
His book, *The Good Great Place*, was instrumental in fram-
ing a philosophy of environment upon which Starbucks
has built itself.

Not everyone spends their time at a coffee shop,
though. And yet, there are still places of socialization and
community building that most of us frequent. They just
look different. Upon graduating from college, I took a
youth pastorate position at a church in a small town in
Ohio. The closest Starbucks at the time was at least 30
minutes away and completely out of the city limits. None

---

[16] See Kunstler's book *The Geography of Nowhere*.

of the students or people from Wadsworth regularly socialized there. But they did have their own third place. During the fall, it was at the local high school football stadium where the whole city would gather to watch the games, socialize, and catch up on life together. In the winter, it was the school basketball games. Social life and community were built around the school sports schedule.

When I moved to a larger city in California, the dynamic changed. No longer was there one local school to which most of the town sent their children. Now the social environments were more diversified, more spread out and harder to slip into. Yet community had to be found. Instead of it being found in a neighborhood though, the prevalence of the single family home meant that a person could pull into their garage, walk into their home, and never see or talk with a neighbor across the street. The social environment for community wasn't found in the neighborhood, and third places that fostered these social needs were few and far between. It wasn't like one could walk out of their front door, go down the street a block or so and meet up with their mates at the local pub.

Or could they?

We still have these third places in our society today. They don't look like the Italian plazas or the English pubs, but they do exist. They are the coffee shops, hair salons, fitness gyms, bookstores, greasy-spoon diners, civic clubs, recreational centers, and social environments of our society. They are the places, distinct from our homes and offices, where we spend much time relating to others in one fashion or another. In some ways, they are the local places that are unique to your city. While national chains can be found providing a similar franchised experience in every town, these third places are the unique local spots special to your town. They provide an experience that can be had nowhere else, with a menu, opportunity, and environment that is one of a kind. In my city, it's the places like Espresso To Go Go and The Monarch.

Even though the quality of these "third places" in America isn't on the level of what it is in many European and Asian cities, the third place is still part of our routine lives. Frankly, our need for places to relate and recreate together is essential to our lives. We will always seek to find and develop places where we can hang out, have a drink together, share stories, laugh, and relate together. Humans will always need third places. Why is that?

Image-Bearing Community

What makes us relational beings? Why do we enjoy spending time with other humans? Some might point to nature and tell us that the biological manner of child reproduction and the subsequent care for the young preconditions us to instinctively gravitate toward other humans. While a certain element of this rings true, it doesn't seem that biology or nature really fully answer this question. I have yet to see a family of spiders build friendships with other spiders and hang out together at a sports bar celebrating a birthday. Maybe I missed it.

No, it seems that we were made for relationship. But it isn't merely because God spoke and implanted some internal sense of duty toward other human beings within us. The prelude to the poetry of creation in Genesis 1:27 is the word of God saying "let us make man in our image."

While this passage doesn't articulate all the details of the Christian doctrine of the Trinity, the initial evidence is there. The nature of God is communal. The Scriptures as a whole display for us the God who is Father, Son, and Holy Spirit. Each person of the Trinity being fully God and uniquely their own person.[17] The Godhead is a community of unity. The Trinity, as Augustine of Hippo contemplated, is a relationship of Lover, Beloved, and Love.[18]

Yet, as man was made to bear the image of God, he could not do that alone. Being a relational creature reflecting a relational Creator without others to relate with would not work. Even as God caused all the animals in the Garden to pass before Adam so that he could name them, the reality sunk in that there was no one like Adam that he could relate with deeply (Gen. 2:19-20). Because God is a relational, communal God, the image he has imprinted on humanity to bear is also a relational, communal image. Community had to be formed.

And so God gave the first man, Adam, a companion, a friend, a lover, a person whom he could relate to and build community with. From the start, our inherent nature is that we are created to relate to one another. Even the most reclusive introvert still needs relationship with others. We were created for community.

---

[17] e.g. Matthew 1:16-17 recounts the Father speaking at the Son's baptism as the Spirit descended. John 1:1-3 tells us that Christ, the Word of God was *with* God and *was* God. Acts 5:3-4 says that lying against the Spirit is lying to God.

[18] Augustine of Hippo, "On the Trinity," in *A Select Library of the Nicene and Post-Nicene Fathers of the Christian Church, First Series: St. Augustin: On the Holy Trinity, Doctrinal Treatises, Moral Treatises*, ed. Philip Schaff, trans. Arthur West Haddan, vol. 3 (Buffalo, NY: Christian Literature Company, 1887).

The Prominence of the Third Place

Stephanie wouldn't normally hang out with Summer. It's not that she doesn't like her or that they wouldn't be friends. It's more a problem of proximity. Her life and its unique spectrum of relationships wouldn't necessarily intersect with Summer's. Stephanie lives on the west side of town, Summer lives just slightly east. Stephanie spends her days working with her children at home, while Summer runs her own business and works part time as a nursing assistant at a local hospital. Even their weekend routines are just different enough that the likelihood of the two of them being together under the same roof is very slim. Not living or working together makes the job of community formation rather difficult.

This is why the third place is so important in society. It gives people who would not naturally live or work together a place to develop community together. The third place has the potential to build bridges for people of all walks of life to connect and relate in. It becomes a home away from home for people who aren't in the same family to build relationships on a deeper level. It is for this reason that the coffee shop, or hair salon, or bookstore, or farmers market, or library, or pancake house, or recreational center, or any other gathering point for a community is so critical to an ever-present gospel. We are there just as much at times as we are anywhere else, and we are there with a different community of people than we would be anywhere else.

The Church and the Third Place

One might ask what sphere of life the church belongs in. When I was a teenager and would go to visit my grandparents, I often found their circle of relationships and life centered around the church. We were there on Sunday morning, Sunday evening, Wednesday evening, Saturday mornings, and every other time the lights were on and the doors were open. My grandparents' closest friends were members of the local church. In the realm of a largely Christianized society, the church, as a place, became an identifiable member within the category of third places. But times have changed. Christianity no longer holds the significant cultural relevance that it used to and as a result, the church building, by and large, is not the predominate third place that it used to be.

But another shift has taken place as well, a cultural shift. As the influence of Christianity in our culture has diminished and even been significantly marginalized, the church has had to rediscover her mission and reassess her methodologies in accomplishing that mission. The mission of the church has constantly been to "make disciples of all nations" (Matt. 28:19) by pointing a dying world to the relocating good news of Christ and him crucified. By necessity, the mission of the church has always required Christians to be in the presence of non-Christians, declaring the good news of life in Jesus. While the mission has never changed, the method in accomplishing that mission has.

I was there for the last one. During my eight-year tenure at Santa Rosa Bible Church, I often heard of the fantastic impact the annual Western Night had on the community. For over thirty years, the high quality, engaging, and culturally relevant show had brought in thousands of people and introduced them to the gospel. I've heard the stories and met several people that were brought to Christ through the outreach of the Western Night. I caught a glimpse of the response cards and numbers of people that came to Christ through these events. But in 2004, the audience wasn't huge. Nor was the auditorium filled with a majority of unbelievers either. More or less it was people from the church that remembered what a great event it was, enjoyed it, and came to reminisce about old times.

For previous generations, the methodology of mission that invited people to come to a church building worked. The church building was a legitimate third place. But today that methodology isn't as effective. Non-Christians aren't as likely to come to a church worship service, let alone some Christian entertainment event. Instead, today a methodology shift has to be in effect. We must change our view of the church in relationship to these third places. The church isn't just another third place alongside your local hair salon or coffee shop or community club. The church is a distinct people (not place) sent to bear witness to Christ in the everyday places of our society, including the third places. (1 Pt. 2:9-10).

The Gospel at Work in the Third Places

Why do I frequent the coffee shop on Douglas and St. Francis every day? For one reason, it's really good coffee. For another reason, I get to meet people I wouldn't normally meet because I hang out there. The owners have created a place that is inviting and warm. It's a place that you want to spend your day. Since this coffee shop opened in the early part of the year, I've become familiar with the owners, their staff, and many of the frequent customers to the shop. I've been invited to parties and dinners with people that I wouldn't normally have the opportunity to spend time with. I've been able to pray for the concerns and anxieties of the people I see day in and day out. I am continually asking God to give me opportunities to specifically speak about Christ to their lives and situations. I'm not looking for a pulpit to be brought into the store and for me to be able to preach a sermon in the midst of the other patrons. I am looking for relationships to be built so that there is enough shared-life occurring that it will raise questions in others about the way I live my life and will allow me to dialogue with them about Christ.

The ever-present gospel in the third place means that Christians need to be in these places. We've tried our best to create a Christian culture that contains Christian music, Christian literature, Christian gyms, Christian coffee shops, and distinct Christian clubs. Instead of living in and interacting with the culture around us for the sake of the gospel, we've abandoned the third places to create our own where non-Christians don't exist.

By being present in these places and displaying a life that has been created by God for relationship and community with others, we show the uniqueness of a God of love. We show the dislocation and brokenness of our own lives. Consequently, because of that brokenness, we also get to show the act of confession, repentance, and faith as genuine responses to the good news of a King who was dislocated for us so that we could be relocated in Him. We get to show a life of renovation to those who wouldn't see it if we merely told them to come to a church building. An ever-present gospel in these third places requires that we actually be present in places like these. Frequent a coffee shop. Join a book club. Get a gym membership. Find third places and become a regular.

Showing the King in the Third Places

But showing up isn't enough. There is a distinct way we must live in those third places to show that we are citizens of a different kingdom. Peter speaks to this when he says,

> *Dear friends, I warn you as "temporary residents and foreigners" to keep away from worldly desires that wage war against your very souls. Be careful to live properly among your unbelieving neighbors. Then even if they accuse you of doing wrong, they will see your honorable behavior, and they will give honor to God when he judges the world. (1 Pt. 2:11–12)*

Peter calls us, as citizens of another kingdom, to a clear distinction in the way we live. On the one hand, in regard to ourselves, we are to pursue holiness and fight sin. We are to strive for holiness and godliness in our attitudes and conduct. On the other hand, in regard to our neighbors, we are to live honorably in the way we speak, act, and conduct ourselves with them. To say it another way, we are to live with moral excellence and beauty toward those we interact with in the third places. Why must we live this way?

Peter says that ultimately, by seeing our lives, they will give honor to God as the King. We are to display the character and conduct of the King who the world will one day acknowledge as King over all. The judgment day may be too late for them to repent and turn from their sin, but the testimony of our lives will be a constant witness to them of the King, leaving them with no excuse. This means that we should live so well in the midst of the world that we are, by our lifestyle, announcing the King that we serve and the Kingdom to which we belong.

The Presence of Mind to Be Present

One practical way that this type of love expresses itself is by our presence with others when we are actually with them. It seems to be the case more and more that whenever my wife and I go out on a date, we notice other couples in the room sitting at the same table staring intently into the world wide web on their cell phone. The glow of the smart-device covers their face and the concentration and devotion they exhibit towards whatever they are looking at is obvious. However, it looks rather odd to see two people at the same table starting into two devices and sending a significant amount of time not talking to one another. I often wonder if they are unable to talk and send one another text messages to communicate. It seems that this sort of ailment is occurring more and more these days. I, for one, am not innocent myself.

The everPresent Gospel in Third Places: Social Environments

In reflecting on the implications of the gospel in the third places, we would do well to love one another and give to one another our full and constant attention. As Kingdom citizens, we display the patient, listening ear of the King as we listen and patiently involve ourselves in the lives of those sitting across the table from us. While some might call this "active listening," I call it actually being where you are. Just as our heavenly Father listens to us and answers to help us (2 Cor. 6:2), so we reflect his presence with us as we listen and answer well those we are in conversation with.

This takes a bit of work and discipline on our part. It means putting aside any and all distraction, paying careful attention to the words, intentions, and thoughts behind what our friends are saying. It actually means being quiet and stopping our speech. It is sad to me that one of the problems that plagues so many ministries and leaders today isn't the content that they put out; it's the fact that they aren't quiet enough to stop speaking and to listen. Whenever there is a event within our culture that raises questions, the evangelical blogosphere and social media machine explodes. Everyone is quick to post a response, an opinion or a critique within milliseconds of the event occurring. Yet the wisdom that James calls for in being "quick to listen, slow to speak" is nowhere to be found (Jas. 1:19).

I wonder how many of our non-Christian friends won't engage serious matters with us because we won't hear them out before formulating our responses and speaking judgement down upon them? If we are serious about being present with them and displaying the nature of the King and his Kingdom, we must give serious effort to the work of listening. Do we pay attention to their words, ask good questions of their thinking, listen to what they are actually saying and take the time and effort to learn them. This is what being present fully feels like. It's putting others first to the extent that we can hear, know, and feel with them what they are struggling and wrestling with. It's not merely listening for fallacies in their thinking to plug with ethical mandates into so they will look and think and behave like us. It's showing the care of a shepherd who loves his flock and gives himself for them.

There are a myriad of other practical ways that this demonstrates itself in everyday life. This kind of kingdom life is evidenced by a life of grace - showing unearned kindness toward others. How do you show unearned kindness toward others? You give of yourself for the blessing of others. You serve and give and show grace. You live and speak and act in such a way to show the value and glory of the King and his Kingdom. The ethic for Kingdom citizens in this place is grace. "Freely you have received; freely give" (Matt. 10:8).

Questions for Group Discussion:

1. What current "third places" can you identify in your city or town? What makes them attractive to be in?
2. What is the relationship between the church and third places? Does your local church attempt to function more like a third place or does it send people out to inhabit the third places?
3. How can we practically build community and live amongst the world in the third places? How do third places allow us access to others we wouldn't normally come in contact with?
4. What is the importance of listening and showing grace to those who differ with us? How does this display the gospel of Christ?

Chapter 8
The everPresent Gospel in Fourth Places: The City

Wichita is an island. Surrounded in every direction by miles and miles of wheat fields, wind mills, and flatlands, an unlikely city has emerged from nowhere. As if to reinforce the city's island identity, a large trench surrounds the city as a moat would a castle, keeping the Arkansas River (pronounced Ar-Kansas here in Wichita) from flooding the city center. I suppose the moat also keeps predators out, too.

It is somewhat difficult to discern why or how a city of Wichita's size would grow up in the middle of nowhere. The river itself isn't the predominate feature like the Mississippi would be to St. Louis or Memphis. The city doesn't sit along a significant major east to west transportation artery of the United States like Oklahoma City or Kansas City do. At one time, it was a stop along a cattle drive trail, but nothing more than a rest stop along a highway of beef. In a lot of ways, I don't understand what brought over half a million residents to one place in the middle of nowhere.

Yet there is some prominence to Wichita. A major United States Air Force base sits off to the southeast of the city. Many of the major global aerospace manufacturers design and build their airplanes here. Because of this, Wichita calls itself the "Air Capital of the World." Additionally, the two highest value, privately owned companies in the United States are based in or have significant offices in Wichita.[19]

Yet there are major problems in Wichita. The city's public schools rank as some of the lowest in the entire state.[20] The city is ranked as one of the top five cities in the US for human trafficking.[21] While the outskirts of the city are financially affluent, the downtown and southern neighborhoods are economically depressed. The racial and socio-economic barriers of the city are easy to discern. Violence and property crime is exceptionally high in the city compared to the rest of the United States.

And yet, given all the problems, Wichita is home to thousands of churches. Religion is on almost every corner of the major streets of Wichita. Over half the population of Sedgwick County (which Wichita overtakes) indicated they were a part of some church in the county.[22] This

---

[19] Cargill and Koch Industries according to Forbes Magazine.
http://www.forbes.com/largest-private-companies/list/ accessed January 5, 2013.

[20] Wichita is ranked #231 out of 244 districts in Kansas.
http://www.schooldigger.com/go/KS/districtrank.aspx, accessed 1/5/14.

[21] http://articles.kwch.com/2010-11-05/wichita-woman_24816984. Accessed 1/5/2014

[22] http://www.thearda.com/rcms2010/r/c/20/rcms2010_20173_county_adh_2010.asp, accessed 1/5/2014.

troubles me, mainly because, as I look at my city and easily see the crime, poverty, pollution, and general disrepair of the city of Wichita and yet half the citizens of this city claim to be Christians, I have to wonder what's going on? How can it be that, in a city where every other resident claims to be a Christian, the nature of the Kingdom isn't really evident?

Based on this evidence, some could point to Christianity itself and quickly declare that it's a bogus system. Skeptics would say that religion doesn't make things better, but that it actually makes things worse. If the world isn't getting any better and my city, with its fifty percent religious rate, isn't a better city because of it, then what is the point? I will concede that; when there is a disparity between what the majority of the people in a place profess to believe and the actual condition of that place, something is off. But I don't believe that the doctrines professed are the things out of place, it's the people.

We've forgotten where we are.

The City of God

Maybe it isn't so much that we've forgotten where we are as much as we've forgotten *who* we are. Yes, we are people who live in time and space, but who are we really in regard to this world? Who are we in regard to the cities that we inhabit? If we can correctly identify who we are, then our manner of life where we are will be different.

Peter is exceptional at helping us along in this. He writes:

You are a chosen race, a royal priesthood, a
holy nation, a people for his own possession,

that you may proclaim the excellencies of him who called you out of darkness into his marvelous light. Once you were not a people, but now you are God's people; once you had not received mercy, but now you have received mercy. Beloved, I urge you as sojourners and exiles to abstain from the passions of the flesh, which wage war against your soul. (1 Pt. 2:9–11)

These words are ripe with identity. Take a moment and examine the words that Peter uses to describe the dispersed Christian family he is writing to. He calls them "a chosen race" and "a royal priesthood." They are a "holy nation" and "a people for [God's] own possession." Bringing to mind the ancient Scriptures of Hosea, Peter reminds them that, at one time, they were homeless and unidentified as "not a people" but now they are "God's people." They were once strangers to God's love and mercy and "had not received mercy, but *now* you have received mercy." All of this is summed up in the identifying statement, "beloved." This is who we are if we are in Christ. We are God's people. We are his beloved. We are chosen, adopted, accepted, holy priests for Him. We are his people.

If this is who we are then how does this answer the first question? Where are we? From those identities, Peter instructs us as to where we are, but he does it once again by reminding us of who we are. Because we are loved by God, because we are his and belong to him, because we have received mercy and grace from him, Peter now calls us sojourners and exiles.

Not Where We Want To Be

I admit, those two identities can be disturbing. We want to be home, we want to feel relaxed and comfortable. We want to be in our element. But Peter is telling us that we aren't there. Sojourning brings to mind wandering. Like Bilbo Baggins on an epic journey that will take us "there and back again," for many the concept of being a sojourner isn't appealing. Furthermore, to remind us that we are "exiles" doesn't help the case. An exile is a refugee; someone who has been rejected from the place they used to inhabit. To be called an exile affirms the fact that we aren't where we want to be.

Maybe this answers our questions. Maybe the dilemma of our cities is solved by realizing that they aren't our homes, they aren't where we are supposed to be, and because of that, they don't really matter. After all, didn't the writer of Hebrews affirm the saints of old for acknowledging they were only on a temporary visa to this planet while they waited and anticipated a greater, better city? Faith, it seems, should take its cues from Abraham and reject this forsaken place and live for a better city, a better place. Let the drug lords and mob bosses have the cities. We have a better home. Jesus is off building it for us right now. When he comes back, this place will be nuked by his glory and our heavenly city will come down from heaven, ready for us to dwell in.

Maybe this sounds well and good to you, but it sounds rather unfortunate and sad to me, not because I have some utopian view of Wichita, nor because I view it as a particularly spectacular place. What troubles me about this sort of thinking is that it presents another awful division to how we see life. People of faith, so it's argued, are living for the "sweet by and by" that is heavenly. The people of this world are living for the here and now that is earthly. Logically, it would follow that faith-people could care less about earth-people and their cities. It's the same spiritual/material dichotomy that we discussed in chapter four.

Wasted Service

Perhaps this division exists in our minds because we hate to be wasteful.

One Wednesday evening, the families that make up my Gospel Community recognized that a local park we like to take our children to play at was overwhelmed with litter. As an act of service to our city and our neighbors, we went to the park with trash bags and spent several hours picking up garbage. Everyone in the group, including our children, was involved in the clean-up. After a few hours, we had picked up an enormous amount of trash but as we surveyed the park, we felt like we had hardly made a dent. A few weeks later, I took my kids to the park to play and it was as if we never worked there at all. My daughter asked what had happened and was reasonably frustrated that people had not taken care of the park she loved to play in so much. In some ways, I felt like we had wasted an evening trying to serve our city.

It is this sort of seemingly frustrating waste that drives us crazy. The work in the park was a futile effort. When we look at our cities and our attempts to better them, we might feel that our efforts are in vain. Trying to reform the criminals, feed the poor, clean up the graffiti, and rebuild the condemned houses are largely ineffective. There is always crime. The homeless don't get jobs or become fiscally responsible. Buildings still stand vacant. Garbage continues to pile up in our parks. Working for the good of our cities here on this earth seems to be a big waste. Things aren't getting any better.

Because of this we might think that, since this isn't our home, since we are "sojourners" and "exiles," we don't have any responsibility or any real impact to make on this earth. We are, in fact, waiting for a better city (Heb. 11:10, 16). We don't expect the emergence of a utopian society on this current earth, but look instead for a new heavens and a new earth (Rev. 21:1). Because of *who* we are (beloved exiles), we don't have any real relationship to *where* we are, at least not right now.

A Word to Exiles

The exiles of Israel in Jeremiah's day had a similar dilemma. As a nation they had forsaken God's law and abandoned God's ways. As a result, they found themselves taken captive into slavery and exiled from their homes and land. God had sent the Babylonian empire to discipline his people. As they were relocated to a foreign, idolatrous, and strange land, they began to hear that their time there would be short. False prophets were telling the nation that God would deliver them quickly and that getting settled was foolish. Certainly God wouldn't want his people to endure living in a pagan place.

However, God's word to these exiles was quite different than that of the false prophets.

*"Thus says the Lord of hosts, the God of Is-
rael, to all the exiles whom I have sent into
exile from Jerusalem to Babylon: Build houses
and live in them; plant gardens and eat their
produce. Take wives and have sons and
daughters; take wives for your sons, and give
your daughters in marriage, that they may
bear sons and daughters; multiply there, and
do not decrease. But seek the welfare of the
city where I have sent you into exile, and pray
to the Lord on its behalf, for in its welfare you
will find your welfare." (Jer. 29:4–7)*

The message was astounding. Not only was God telling them to settle down and get used to being in Babylon,
but he was telling them he had *sent* them to that very hostile and ungodly place. The instruction God gave to the
exiles of Israel is exactly how he would have us live in the
cities in which we are "exiles" today.

Exiled Life in the City

At first blush, this sort of instruction sounds rather
unglamorous. There's nothing about taking over the po-
litical system or starting a revolution. No word about gen-
erating a resistance of any kind or staging a cultural war
to demonstrate the superiority of righteousness. Even the
radical spiritual nature of this way of life is apparently
lacking. To be quite honest, what God tells the exiles to do
is rather mundane.

Consider the list:
- Build houses and live in them.
- Plant gardens and eat their produce.

- Marry off your children so they have children and multiply as a family.
- Seek the good of the city.
- Pray for the good of the city.

This list seems so ordinary that we might overlook it as having any benefit for us. Could it have any real value for those of us trying to impact and change our cities for the sake of the King? Could this sort of life have any solid impact in demonstrating the renovating reality of the Kingdom?

Consider with me for just a moment what makes a city a city. Whether you live in a large metropolis or a small rural town, consider what elements constitute that place. Cities, large or small, are a collection of homes, work environments, and social spaces. In essence, cities are concentrated densities of first, second, and third places.

The gospel lived in the first places requires a home, so God says build houses and live there. The gospel lived in the first places challenges us to be cultivators of life, so we marry, have kids, and raise them to know the King. Multiply a kingdom. The gospel lived in second places diligently cultivates the world the King has made, so we plant gardens, cultivating and tending them, enjoying the fruits of our labor. The gospel lived in third places develops community and friendship with others. It works to develop cultures of grace, kindness, and hospitality. It seeks the good of the of the neighbor, so we must be with others, spending time in the midst of the world, hanging out in a coffee shop and making new friends.

How does the gospel take root and change our cities? It's by sojourners and exiles living everyday, ordinary lives as Kingdom citizens in the various places that constitute a city. It's nothing overtly dramatic or massively amazing. It's everyday life present where we are; whether at home, at work, or at the park. It doesn't take a seminary degree or a profound religious experience. You don't have to have a church building to see the Kingdom advance in your city. God calls you wherever you are at, in the suburban town or the small village or the center of the largest city on earth, to live for the King by seeking the welfare of that place in all the places you are present.

Sent Sojourners

I don't feel particularly attached to Wichita. Honestly, as a place, I liked Santa Rosa, California a whole lot better. It was California, after all. The weather was always perfect. There was a perfect mix of redwood forest and beautiful vineyards. It was thirty minutes from the coast and just a few hours from the mountains. The hills rolled with beautiful green grass in the spring and in the summer months they were golden. In the summer, the heat would rise during the day and then about six o'clock in the evening, a blanket of fog would roll in from the coast and cool off everything. I loved Santa Rosa.

But now I live in the prairie-lands of the Midwest. The snow and cold have set in and chilled me to the bone. Unpredictable hailstorms have taken their toll on my minivan. The summer heat can be unbearable. There are no mountains to be found. The city itself isn't that attractive or culturally important. It seems like five steps down on the ladder of paradise places that I've lived in. But here I am. And the word of Jeremiah 29:4 tells me why I'm here. I've been sent.

As a reminder to us of our place in whatever city we live in, the Lord spoke to the exiled Israelites, and speaks to us as well, and says "Thus says the Lord of hosts, the God of Israel, to all the exiles *whom I have sent"* (Jer. 29:4). Why are you where you are? Why has the Father poured out wonders of love and grace and mercy upon you? Why has he come to relocate your broken life? It's because he has sovereignly sent you to live as his Kingdom people. He has placed you in the city to live an ordinary, everyday life as a citizen of the City of God, inviting others to the King.

The everPresent Gospel Every Place

What would it be like in our cities if the gospel was displayed and declared by sent exiles? How would a city change over the course of generations if we intentionally lived, multiplied, and raised children, grand-children, even great-grandchildren for the king? How would a city change as industrious, laboring workers engaged the office, working for the King himself? What would a city look like as the Kingdom citizens inhabited the social environments of their city to know, serve, and love their neighbors? How would things be different?

We might think that we would never know the full extent of this vision. In some sense in the here and now that is true. But the King means to bring all things into submission under him. At his glorious and righteous return, the reality of this vision will be fulfilled. The city of

God will be realized as the King sits on the throne and the Kingdom brought to bear on every place encapsulating people from everywhere. A new heaven and a new earth will be realized as Jesus finally renovates all things for his glory. What began in the seed-bed Garden of Eden and was dislocated and distorted will finally be relocated and renovated in the City-Kingdom of God. The dwelling place of God will once again be with man "and they will be his people, and God himself will be with them" (Rev. 21:3).

But while we wait for this vision to be fully consummated, we are sent as exiles into the world to live and bear witness to the King. He sends us to every place, to every people to demonstrate a life with him leading our way. Our lives are temporary and finite. We're fixed in space and place so that in this unique, one of a kind place we can display his glory. Be it the café on Bitting, the park down the street, my eighty-something year-old house, the aerospace company hanger, or any other traveled place, this place is God's place. Seeing that moves mountains.

Where are you?

Questions for Group Discussion:

1. What makes your city or town unique? Discuss the culture, demographics and design of your city.
2. How does our identity as "aliens and strangers" inform the way in which we view and live in our cities?
3. How will being kingdom citizens living ordinary lives in our cities impact the city for the glory of God?
4. Do you see yourself as being sent to the city in which you live? How will that impact the way in which you live in your city?

About the Author

 **Jeremy Writebol** (@jwritebol) is the husband of Stephanie and daddy of Allison and Ethan. He lives and works in Wichita, KS as the Community Pastor at Journey the Way and the director of Porterbrook Kansas. He is a graduate of Moody Bible Institute and The Resurgence Training Center. Catch up with him at jwritebol.net.

Other Resources
from GCD Books

Visit GCDiscipleship.com

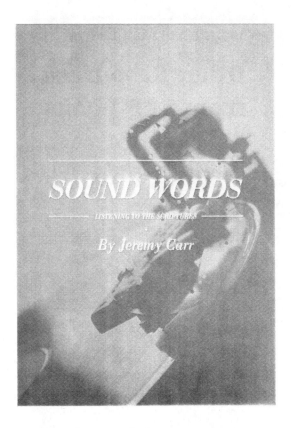

Sounds Words by Jeremy Carr

"The church continues to need an understanding of discipleship that draws people to love and know God. This book delivers. It is an accessible and practical theology of scripture for discipleship. Jeremy is not exhorting you to love the Bible more, but declaring that God's love for you causes you to know and love him and his Word more."

JUSTIN S. HOLCOMB
Adjunct Professor of Theology and
Philosophy, Reformed Theological Seminary

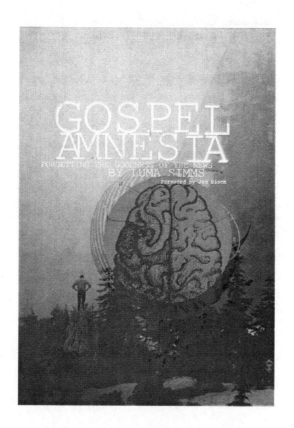

Gospel Amensia by Luma Simms

"Luma Simms remembers vividly what it was like to be simply going through the motions of a spiritual life. She writes like someone who has just been awakened from a nightmare and can still describe it in detail. Luma's voice communicates the pain of forgetting what matters most, and may be just the voice to reach the half-awake."

FRED SANDERS
Associate Professor of Theology,
Torrey Honors Institute, Biola University

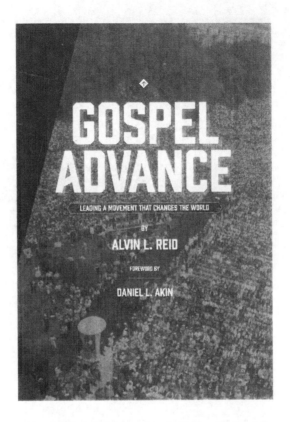

Gospel Advance by Alvin L. Reid

"*Gospel Advance* is Alvin Reid's challenge to the Church to recover our mission focus and advance a movement of God through the gospel. Reading this book is like sitting down across from this passionate evangelism professor and hearing from his heart. He describes the history of evangelical awakenings and prescribes a way forward for 21st century believers. May the Lord use this work to ignite your heart for the nations!"

TREVIN WAX
Managing Editor of *The Gospel Project*
author of *Counterfeit Gospels*

CPSIA information can be obtained at www.ICGtesting.com
Printed in the USA
LVOW07s2237070116

469670LV00021B/1514/P